Research in Teaching and Learning
Gwen Lloyd

Volume 3

STUDENTS' THOUGHT PROCESSES

Merlin C. Wittrock

TEACHERS' THOUGHT PROCESSES

Christopher M. Clark
Penelope L. Peterson

A PROJECT OF THE
AMERICAN EDUCATIONAL RESEARCH ASSOCIATION

MACMILLAN PUBLISHING COMPANY
A Division of Macmillan, Inc.
NEW YORK

Collier Macmillan Publishers
LONDON

Macmillan Publishing Company
866 Third Avenue, New York, N.Y. 10022

Collier Macmillan Canada, Inc.

Library of Congress Catalog Card Number: 90-33385

Printed in the United States of America

printing number
1 2 3 4 5 6 7 8 9 10

Library of Congress Cataloging-in-Publication Data

Research in teaching and learning : a project of the American
    Educational Research Association.
        p.   cm.
    Chapters from the Handbook of research on teaching.
    Includes bibliographical references.
    Contents: 1. Paradigms and programs / Lee S. Shulman —
2. Quantitative methods / Robert L. Linn. Qualitative methods /
Frederick Erickson — 3. Students' thought processes / Merlin C.
Wittrock. Teachers' thought processes / Christopher M. Clark,
Penelope L. Peterson — 4. Mathematics / Thomas A. Romberg, Thomas
P. Carpenter. Natural sciences / Richard T. White, Richard P.
Tisher.
    1. Education—Research—United States. 2. Teaching.   I. Shulman,
Lee S.   II. American Educational Research Association.
III. Handbook of research on teaching.
LB1028.25.U6R47   1990
370'.7'8073—dc20   90-33385
                                                          CIP

CONTENTS

STUDENTS' THOUGHT PROCESSES

TEACHERS' THOUGHT PROCESSES

EDITORIAL NOTE

I want to thank all the people who participated in the creation of the *Handbook of Research on Teaching*. Because of their efforts the *Handbook* continues from its publication in 1986 to receive an overwhelming reception from the world-wide community of researchers and educators interested in the study of teaching.

Because of the exceptional interest in the use of the *Handbook* in the classroom, we have selected several of its chapters for separate publication in Series *Research in Teaching and Learning*. Each volume of the Series consists of closely related chapters, or of a single chapter, on a theme of particular interest to the readers of the *Handbook*. I hope that the publication of the volumes of this series will further enhance the contributions of the *Handbook of Research on Teaching* to the community of researchers, teachers, and students interested in the study of teaching.

Merlin C. Wittrock
January 30, 1990

STUDENTS' THOUGHT PROCESSES

Merlin C. Wittrock

The recent research on students' thought processes studies the effects of teachers and instruction upon the student perceptions, expectations, attentional processes, motivations, attributions, memories, generations, understandings, beliefs, attitudes, learning strategies, and metacognitive processes that mediate achievement. The recent study of these student thought processes brings a distinctive perspective to the understanding of teachers' effects upon learning, the development of theories of teaching, and the design and analysis of teaching (Doyle, 1977, 1980; Winne & Marx, 1980; Wittrock, 1978). The distinctive perspective emphasizes the critical role that student background knowledge, perceptions of instruction, attention to the teacher, motivation and attribution for learning, affective processes, and ability to generate interpretations and understandings of instruction play in teaching and in influencing student achievement.

In contrast to research that studies how teachers or instructional processes directly contribute to student achievement, research on students' thought processes examines how teaching or teachers influence what students think, believe, feel, say, or do that affects their achievement. As a result the research designs of these studies include measures of at least two consecutive and reciprocally related links between teaching and student achievement. The first link is between teaching and student cognition. The second link is between student cognition and learning or achievement. There can often be additional links, and they can be related to one another in complex ways, such as the reciprocal relations that exist among student thoughts, achievement, and teaching. But the distinctive characteristic of the research on students' thought processes is the idea that teaching affects achievement through student thought processes. That is, teaching influences student thinking. Students' thinking mediates learning and achievement.

Perhaps teaching can also directly influence achievement, just as learning can sometimes occur without awareness. But research on students' cognitive processes examines and tests the utility of assuming otherwise, that teaching can better be

The author thanks reviewers Penelope Peterson (University of Wisconsin—Madison) and Walter Doyle (University of Texas Austin) for their excellent suggestions.

understood, and improved, by knowing its effects upon the learners' thoughts that mediate achievement.

To give these statements more concrete meaning and to introduce the research findings that follow in the next sections, we will briefly discuss three often reported findings that relate teaching directly to student achievement. With each example we will contrast a simple input–output explanation of the findings with a model that interjects student thought processes as mediators between the teaching and the achievement.

First, the controversial self-fulfilling prophecy, that high or low teacher expectations regarding student achievement lead, respectively, to higher or lower student school achievement and to higher or lower student self-preceptions of academic ability, seems often, but not always, to be found in relevant empirical studies. To explore and to try to explain this phenomenon, research studies that examine student thought processes ask the following questions about the mediators of achievement. Did the teachers convey their expectations to the students? Did the students perceive the teachers' expectations? Did the students attempt to change their behavior or their self-concepts in response to the teachers' expectations? Were the students able to change their learning patterns, motivations, and expectations in response to the teaching? Did achievement change in response to these altered student cognitive and affective processes?

Research on students' thinking predicts that if these changes occurred in students' thinking, then the self-fulfilling prophecy would occur. The model implies that some students in a classroom might show these changes in thinking while other students might not show them, resulting in a teacher expectancy effect only for some students, a finding commonly reported in the literature. Another implication of this model is that the individual student, or the dyad, the teacher and the student, not the classroom, is the preferred unit to use to study the teacher expectancy effect. The reason is that student thoughts in response to the same teacher expectations differ from one learner to another.

Second is the often reported finding that teacher praise or reward increases learning. With this finding, a perspective that emphasizes students' thinking leads us to examine the interpretations and attributions that students construct from these rewards. To what extent do students perceive the rewards, and to what extent can students increase their information-processing skills to improve their achievement in response to the praise or reward? If students do not attribute the rewards to their own actions, or to activities over which they have some control, we would not expect the rewards to enhance learning. Teacher praise may also provide information about classroom performance to all the students who observe another student receive the praise. Praise of one student might mediate learning among a large number of students through its informational, as well as its motivational qualities. In brief, learning from teaching is not automatic. It occurs primarily through active and effortful information processing by students who must perceive and interpret teachers' actions for them to influence achievement.

Third, the time teachers allocate to learning has frequently been found to correlate directly with student achievement. The study of student cognitive processes, in this context, leads to the following hypotheses. The students' constructive use of the time, not the time per se, affects learning and achievement. Consequently, time actually devoted to the task by the students should correlate with learning more highly than should time allocated to the task by the teacher. In addition, attention, if accurately reported by the learners, should correlate with learning more highly than should time devoted to the task, as measured by observers in the classroom. The reason is that attention is an internal cognitive process that is not equivalent to externally observable activities, such as time spent looking at a book, or out a classroom window. Both of these findings are also supported in the literature on students' perceptions of attention, which will be discussed later in this chapter under the heading "Students' Perceptions of Cognitive Processes in the Classroom."

Those three examples introduce a perspective underlying the studies presented in the following sections. The following sections of this chapter illustrate but do not exhaust research on student thought processes that mediate achievement. These student thought processes include an awareness or perception of teaching, attention to it, motivation to learn, and ability to generate relations between knowledge and experience, on the one hand, and the materials or concepts to be learned, on the other hand.

These topics are discussed next. In addition, research on the teaching of learning strategies and metacognitive processes, which emphasizes awareness and control of student learning processes, is also briefly discussed. Again, the chapter introduces and illustrates the research but cannot in these few pages discuss all of the research studies in these extensive areas. Research in these areas is important for understanding how students learn how to learn and how students can be taught to improve their thought processes to facilitate knowledge acquisition, learning, and memory. Together these student thought processes and strategies comprise an organized and complementary set of cognitions. The discussion of these student thought processes represents an answer to the problem of how students' thoughts mediate learning from teaching.

Students' Perceptions and Expectations

Research on students' thought processes promises to enhance understanding of teaching and its outcomes by providing information about the instruction as it is experienced by the learners. The instruction experienced by the learners may be different from the intended instruction; or the instruction may not be understood or perceived by the learners. In these research studies, the learners' perception of the teaching is the functional instruction that influences student learning and achievement.

In the following paragraphs we begin to analyze the thought processes that contribute to the students' experience and understanding of teaching.

Students' Academic Self-Concepts and Expectations

From the beginning of elementary school, children uniformly and positively perceive their academic performance (Stipek, 1981). They often exaggerate their academic ability, using absolute rather than relative standards to evaluate their performances. As early as the first grade, high-achieving, compared with low-achieving, boys have higher expectations for success in school (Stipek & Hoffman, 1980). In the third or fourth grade, the children's perceived school performance begins to correlate positively with their teachers' estimates of their ability. By the sixth grade, children's perceived academic ability becomes more realistic and related to the performance of their classmates (Nicholls, 1979).

Teachers' feedback to children regarding their school performance seems to be related to the development of children's self-concept of ability. Kindergarten and first graders rated their own intelligence by their effort and ability to follow directions, while second and third graders emphasized their performance on specific subject matter tasks (Stipek, 1981).

These self-evaluations of ability seem to reflect the feedback the teachers often used at these grade levels. From these data, it seems that young children are capable of perceiving feedback from teachers regarding their academic performances and those of their peers in school. These perceptions also seem to influence their expectations about their future school performances.

It is too early to know the generality of these findings. But the findings suggest the early and definite effects teachers can have upon students' expectations and self-concepts of school ability.

*Students' Perception of Schools,
Teachers, and Teachers' Behaviors*

Students also perceive school factors related to achievement, including differences among teachers and among teacher behaviors. Paton, Walberg, and Yeh (1973) found that many minority children in high school felt that they had the ability to learn. But these same children felt that luck determined achievement in school. The children felt that somebody blocked them from success, even though they had the ability to learn. These results agree with the data of the Coleman report (1966), where the feeling among students of lack of environmental control accounted for more variance in academic achievement than did any other variable.

Brookover, Beady, Flood, Schweitzer, and Wisenbaker (1977) report a related finding in the elementary school. They measured student perceptions of academic climates, and found that the belief that it was futile to pursue success in school contributed more than any other comparable variable to the variance in achievement.

These global affective processes merit further study to determine their causes, and to determine more precisely how these beliefs produce effects upon students' achievements in school. Again, the attributions students make about achievement and the sense of control they experience over their destiny in school seem to be powerful cognitive processes that mediate their school performances.

Students' perceptions of their teachers, teaching processes, and the differential treatments learners receive from teachers seem to mediate achievement in school. About at age 7, children often begin to develop more abstract and deeper perceptions of people that are based on consistent qualities that transcend observable behavior (Livesley & Bromley, 1973). Several studies have examined the qualities of a good teacher that are perceived by students. Although there is controversy over these findings, some studies find students choosing teachers who are warm, friendly, supportive and communicative, while, at the same time, orderly, highly motivating, and in charge of classroom discipline (e.g., Beck, 1967). See Weinstein (1983) for further discussions of these topics.

Students seem to discriminate differential treatments teachers give them in the classroom. In research on the teacher expectancy phenomenon, or so-called self-fulfilling prophecy, several studies examined whether students perceive differential treatment in the classroom between high- and low-achieving male students. Weinstein and Middlestadt (1979) asked two groups of children, Grades 1–3 and Grades 4–6, to rate 60 teacher behaviors as applicable or not applicable to fictional high and low achievers, The children perceived teachers to respond differently to the high achiever and to the low achiever on 15 of the 60 items. The students perceived the teachers as having high expectations and high academic demands for the high-achieving male students, to whom the teachers granted special privileges. The students saw the male low achievers as receiving fewer chances to perform in class, but as receiving greater teacher interest and concern. The high-achieving males were perceived to be more popular, friendly, competitive, attentive, independent, and successful than the low-achieving males.

In a later study, Weinstein, Marshall, Brattesani, and Middlestadt (1982) examined the perceptions of over 200 fourth through sixth graders regarding teacher behaviors toward fictional male and female high and low achievers in school. The elementary school students perceived the male and female low achievers as receiving more direction, rules, work, and negative feedback than did the male and female high achievers, whom they perceived as receiving higher teacher expectations for performance and success, more freedom of choice, and greater opportunities. Cooper and Good (1982) report that students for whom teachers had high expectations described themselves as receiving less frequent criticism and more frequent praise than did students for whom teachers had low expectations.

Cooper (1979) presents a model, which is elaborated with some relevant data in another paper (Cooper, 1983), of the teacher expectancy effect, as mediated by student thought processes, and as studied by Weinstein and her colleagues in the two papers just described. Cooper's model suggests that high teacher expectation students frequently receive positive feedback contingent upon their effort, while students with low teacher expectations receive more noneffort-contingent negative feedback as a way to control their behavior, which teachers see as less likely to result in learning but more likely to result in classroom disturbances. As a result, low teacher expectation students are less likely to come to believe in the value of effort for attaining success in class, and therefore, to show less persistence and to experience less success. (See Cooper & Good, 1982 for further discussion.)

From these studies, it is clear that students perceive expectations by teachers and differentiate classroom treatment given to high and low expectation students. The differential treatments may induce different self-concepts of ability and different attributional patterns among students. The data on this latter issue are not extensive enough to warrant that generalization yet. However, it seems likely that the teacher expectancy effect will not be found by studying whole classrooms. Rather, teachers produce the effect with some students, who perceive differential treatment from teachers, as Weinstein's data show; but teachers may not produce the expectancy effect with other students, who do not perceive the teachers' differential and inappropriate treatment.

Research using the teacher and student dyad as the unit, rather than the classroom as the unit, seems more likely to find the teacher expectancy effect. Students do not all perceive the teacher's actions in the same, or a uniform, way.

For further discussion of these topics, see Amatora, 1952; Ames, 1981; Beam and Horvat, 1975; Blumenfeld, Hamilton,

Bossert, Wessels, and Meece, 1983; Braun, 1976; Brophy, 1983; and Filby and Barnett, 1982.

Students' Perceptions of Teachers' Behavior and Classroom Instructional Processes

Children develop in their understanding of the purposes of instruction and of their teachers' motives behind classroom activities. One study suggests that first graders typically believe that the most important part of their classwork is to get it done, to get to the bottom of the page, or to get to the end of the book (Anderson, 1981). These perceptions by first graders raise fundamental questions about kindergarten and primary school teaching, which sometimes emphasizes the procedural and mechanical aspects of instruction, with less emphasis in understanding the learning involved in the classwork assignments. Are the kindergarten and first grade teachers appropriately teaching the children to focus on the mechanics of instruction, that they need to learn to facilitate understanding later? Or is the development of understanding, which might be of more interest to the pupils, being deferred inappropriately by teaching procedures that focus on behaving correctly but not necessarily on understanding what one is reading or writing in school?

In either case students learn to perceive the goals of instruction as a result of the directions they receive from their teachers. Blumenfeld et al. (1983), in their research on teacher talk and student thought, report a related finding among elementary school students. Teachers' comments and directions about academic performance, including attributions to effort as a way to succeed ("you can do better"), correlated more highly with students' thoughts than did teacher talk about social procedures and about the socialization of the child into the school and society. Apparently the teacher who focuses on the academic work and the students' responsibilities for accomplishing it through effort conveys a sense of the central importance of the intellectual activities. But perceptions of the importance of the social processes of working together are not so readily conveyed by teachers.

Students also perceive the feedback their teachers give them. As I mentioned earlier, students early in elementary school, about second grade, begin to learn from feedback about their own and their peers' relative performances in classrooms (Nicholls, 1978; Stipek, 1981). Consequently, these children learn quickly to rate themselves and their peers as high or low achievers, a consequence of teachers' behaviors that may have effects upon self-concepts, motivations, and attitudes toward peers. Filby and Barnett (1982) studied how elementary school children understand and evaluate one another's reading performance in class. They found about 90% agreement among children regarding which of them were the better readers. "Smooth error-free reading with expression sounds good to everyone" (Filby & Barnett, 1982, p. 444), at least when the whole class had opportunity to hear everyone read aloud.

Teacher praise is perceived by students somewhat differently from the ways it is intended by teachers. Wittrock (1978) distinguished, as have many other authors, two functions of teacher praise and reinforcement. First, there is the *motivational* or reinforcing function of increasing future behavior by appropriately praising or rewarding it. This function does not involve understanding or learning with awareness. Second, there is an *informational* function of teacher praise, which provides feedback about the correctness of a response.

In this much-researched area of teacher praise, the motivational function has long been considered important for teaching children to learn associations well enough to repeat them in future appropriate occasions. To accomplish this motivational or reinforcement function, teacher praise should be used frequently, discriminatively, and contingently.

However, recent classroom research finds that teacher praise does not usually function as a reinforcer or as a motivator. In several studies, Brophy (1981) found that teacher praise did not correlate with other outcomes of teaching, as one would expect if teacher praise functioned as a reinforcer.

In the same article, he also argues that teacher praise is not usually intended as a reinforcer. It is infrequently used by teachers. First grade teachers praised about 11% of the students' correct answers in reading classes (Anderson, Evertson, & Brophy, 1979), and about 10% of the public responses in the junior high school (Evertson, Anderson, Anderson, & Brophy,

1980). In these same two studies teacher praise of student good conduct was much lower, and nearly nonexistent in the first grade.

In these studies, the teachers did not perceive or use praise as it often has been thought they did, that is, as a reinforcer. If praise functioned as a reinforcer, it would be ineffective in the typical classroom, because its infrequent use means that each student would be praised only about once every 2 hours (Brophy, 1981), and because praise is often used noncontingently.

Instead praise seems to function by providing information to all the students who *observe* the student receiving the praise. The information conveys knowledge about the answers, the desired behavior, and the teachers' expectations for performance. These findings also show reasons to study student thought processes rather than studying only direct effects of praise on learners.

Students perceive and respond differently from one another to praise, depending on their intellectual ability, cognitive style, attributions, age, and their desire to please the teacher. Many low-ability students, field-dependent students, external locus students, primary-school students, and students eager to please the teacher respond favorably to praise. For other types of students, praise can be counterproductive, for example, by changing intrinsic motivation to extrinsic motivation (Lepper, 1983) or by changing student attributions for success in school, or their perceptions of their own abilities.

Praise of a high-ability student for success on an easy task may lead to a lower self-concept of ability, or be seen as undeserved by the students. Morine-Dershimer (1982) observed elementary school students' perceptions of teacher praise. Fifty percent of these students perceived the praise to be deserved by themselves, and 23 % of them reported that the praise served an instructional function, such as conveying information about correct answers, encouraging students, and making them feel good. The students high in reading achievement tended to view the praise as deserved by their performance. Students low in reading achievement viewed the praise as serving an instructional function, such as encouraging them or helping them to feel good about learning to read.

Student participation in the classroom discussions also depended upon the pupils' perception of the teachers' intent in using praise. Praise perceived as deserved led to greater participation in classroom discussions. Higher reading-achievement students, and students high in status with teachers and peers, tended to perceive praise as deserved, and also participated more frequently in classroom discussions than did lower reading-ability students. High classroom participation was correlated with reading achievement, after entering reading ability was controlled. Morine-Dershimer (1982) concludes that praise may be perceived by pupils not so much "to *reinforce the individual student* as to *give information to the group*" (p. 432, italics in original). She adds that direct instruction may be effective in that its high proportion of praised correct answers gives the entire class increased information from which all of them can learn.

From these data about perceptions of praise, it seems that praise used by teachers may serve an informational function primarily, rather than a reinforcing function. In addition, it is clear that students perceive this teacher behavior differently from one another and differently, sometimes, from the way teachers intend it to be understood.

These studies of students' perceptions of teachers' classroom behaviors revise our understanding of an important instructional procedure, suggest revisions in the use of praise to increase its informational value, and provide hypotheses about the roles of learners' thought processes in direct instruction.

Students' Perceptions of Cognitive Processes in the Classroom

Wittrock (1978) maintained that before reporting effects of students' thoughts on achievement, studies of students' thought processes in teaching and instruction should show that the students in the research actually performed the cognitive processes intended by the directions, questions, or tasks in the treatments. The students' perceptions of the instruction and teaching may be different from the teachers' intentions. The students may not engage in the thoughts intended by the teachers.

In an extensive series of studies on elementary school students' cognitive processes occuring while learning from teaching, Winne and Marx (1983) examined students' perceptions of classroom instruction and their relation to achievement. They also studied whether students could be trained to use cognitive strategies that would influence instruction. They studied three cognitive processes: (a) orienting, which involved directing students' attention; (b) operating, which included comparing, generating, and using metacognition; and (c) consolidating, which included storage and retrieval. They found that students' perceptions of instruction and the cognitive processes they used in response to it were related to achievement. They also found that they could train cognitive processes, for example through teaching note-taking strategies, that would enhance achievement on objective tests, but not on essay tests.

In another study by these two authors (Winne & Marx, 1980) university students were trained to recognize only, or to recognize and to respond to, the experimental organization or schema for learning from lectures. The learning and use of the experimental schema and the directions to take notes to facilitate learning during a lecture, rather than its recall later, interfered with learning and with the use of the students' customary, previously learned systems for acquiring knowledge during lectures. The students' perception of the new cognitive processes depended upon their previously learned strategies. Learning a new strategy involved modifying a previously learned strategy.

Their results indicate that the new strategy influenced cognitive processing. But the more important finding was that one must know and understand students' perceptions and previously learned strategies in order to teach a new strategy, and to understand how students will respond to it.

These points are elaborated in another paper by Winne and Marx (1982). In this paper they state that there is a lack of a one-to-one correspondence between instruction identified by the teacher and the cognitive processing it cues in the students (p. 513). Observation schedules probably cannot detect the instruction which actually functions for learners. Similar treatments may be perceived as quite different procedures by students, while quite different instructional methods may be perceived as similar by these same students. In addition, students' background knowledge and previously learned strategies influence the perception of teaching.

The direct effects of teacher behaviors, compared with the mediated effects of students' perceptions of the same teachers' behaviors, upon sixth grade students were studied by Stayrook,

Corno, and Winne (1978). Student perceptions of teacher structuring and teacher reacting, but not of teacher soliciting, correlated more highly with achievement in this path-analytic study than did the direct effects of teacher structuring and teacher reacting. These path models did not show statistical significance. However, a reanalysis of the data, reducing error of measurement, improved the significance levels of the data.

These findings imply that research studies should include students' thought processes in their designs. The regularities that exist between teaching and student achievement involve the cognitive transformation performed by the students on the instruction they receive.

In a series of studies Peterson and her colleagues examined students' reports of their cognitive processes occurring during instruction. Peterson, Swing, Braverman, and Buss (1982), also reported in Peterson and Swing (1982), asked fifth and sixth graders, who were shown videotaped segments of their classroom instruction, to describe their thought processes that occurred during the mathematics instruction they viewed on the tapes.

Student-reported attention correlated with success on the mathematics problems more highly than did classroom observers' reports of time-off-task. With ability differences controlled, reports of understanding the lesson also correlated positively with achievement, as did students' reported use of learning strategies, such as relating the problems to experience. Students' ability to determine why and what they understood also correlated with achievement. Students' reports of using specific cognitive strategies, rather than global strategies such as thinking or listening, also correlated with achievement. These specific strategies included "relating information to prior knowledge" and "trying to understand the teacher on problem-level 2" (Peterson et al., 1982, p. 544). Level 2 referred to one of the more difficult types of problems. Last, reported motivational self-thoughts correlated positively with attitudes toward mathematics.

In a related study, using similar procedures with a naturalistic classroom setting and an ethnically and socioeconomically more diverse population of fifth graders, Peterson, Swing, Stark, and Waas (1983) replicated these results and added findings about student affective thoughts during instruction. In this study classroom observation of student engagement in mathematics was unrelated to mathematics achievement, supporting Brophy and Evertson's claim (1976, p. 67) that apparent student attention (observed time-on-task) does not reliably measure anything. Students' negative self-thoughts seemed to lower both student achievement and attitudes. From these studies there is further evidence that student thought processes influence student achievement in the learning of mathematics in elementary schools.

These findings are of interest for several reasons. First, the finding that student reports of attention correlate more highly with mathematics achievement than do observers' reports of time-on-task indicates the importance and utility of obtaining measures of student cognitive processes, even when they involve self-report data. Attention is not the same as observed time-on-task, or time allotted to learning. Second, students are aware of and can recall their cognitive processes accurately enough to predict achievement, at least at a statistically significant level. Third, the more specific cognitive strategies, but not the general strategies. predict achievement. These findings imply that through the study of student thought processes we can discern the effective strategies students use in school learning. With this knowledge teachers can try to teach these strategies to other children.

These classroom studies of student reports of cognitive processes again indicate the utility of studying constructs, such as attention, for refining our understanding of the effects of teaching upon student learning. The latter studies we discussed showed the potential of attention for revising earlier conceptions about time-on-task. In the following section we explore additional implications for teaching that follow from related research literature on attention.

Attention

In the recent research literature, selective attention, voluntary attention, sustained attention, and distractability, among other types of attention, have frequently been studied in laboratories and in school settings (cf. Wittrock, in press). From these studies several components of attention have been identified, including a short-term or phasic, largely involuntary, component, sometimes called arousal or the orienting response, and a long-term or tonic, largely voluntary component. The tonic component, but usually not the phasic component, is involved in learning disabilities, behavior disorders, and in mental retardation (Zeaman & House, 1963).

From recent research on attention, educationally useful, remedial attentional training programs have been developed that help students, including learning-disabled and hyperkinetic learners, to control attention and to enhance learning from teaching. In addition, recent research on attention has led to new explanations of the ways that teacher questions, inserted questions in texts, and objectives given to learners influence classroom learning. In the following paragraphs we will explore these two lines of research, beginning with one study on selective attention, then discussing the recent findings about classroom instructional procedures, questions and objectives, and last discussing attentional training programs for learning disabled, hyperactive, and normal learners.

Willows (1974) gave good and poor readers in the sixth grade distracting words typed in red between the lines of the normal text they were asked to read. Compared with a control group not given the inserted, distracting words, the text in red distracted the poor readers more than it did the good readers. Further, the good readers focused on the meaning of the distracting text, when they did attend to it, while the poor readers focused on the surface structure, the red color of the inserted text. Distractability seems to be a type of attention that sometimes distinguishes good from poor learners.

Other data also implicate attentional problems in some reading disorders. Preston, Guthrie, and Childs (1974) found poor readers in the ninth grade to have a deficit in response to light flashes, but not to words, indicating an attentional deficit, but not an encoding or learning problem. Conners (1976) found similar results regarding reading and attention among third and fourth graders.

In research on adjunct or inserted questions, students are given texts to read with questions inserted either before the paragraphs, called prequestions, or after the paragraphs, called postquestions, that discuss the relevant answers. In these studies, the prequestions usually facilitate verbatim and factual learning, while the postquestions facilitate conceptual learning or learning of information not specific to the question (Boker, 1974).

Prior to the development of attentional models, these results were usually explained by practice, reinforcement, and the opportunity to review paragraphs provided by the postquestions. Wittrock and Lumsdaine (1977) explained these results with an attentional model. They maintained that the prequestions direct the learner's attention to a factual or specific answer. The postquestions, coming after the relevant paragraphs, direct attention only in future paragraphs to the general type of information likely to be asked after the next paragraph is read. Rickards and Denner (1978) and Andre (1979), after reviewing the literature on inserted questions, reached essentially the same conclusion, which is that the questions direct attention, at least among learners who are not already attentive to the text.

In research on the effects of giving students behavioral objectives, an attentional model again has provided a useful explanation of the findings. For many years behavioral objectives given to learners were thought to provide the teachers with readily identifiable behavior that they could easily recognize and immediately and frequently reinforce. However, Duell (1974) tested and found that behavioral objectives function by influencing selective attention. Duchastel (1979) reached the same conclusion in a study in which text of low structural importance was better learned when objectives focused it, directing students away from the text they would otherwise have studied. Kaplan and Simmons (1974) found that objectives given to learners after the text, rather than before, enhanced or broadened the learning to include information related to, but not identical to, the specific answers to the questions. In this study objectives given to learners seem to function somewhat like inserted questions, directing attention. Attention models seem useful for explaining these results and for understanding some of the cognitive effects of questions and objectives.

Attention is a student thought process that may help to explain some of the results found in studies of learning disorders, hyperactivity, and mental retardation. Learning-disabled children show a 2- or 3-year lag in development of selective attention. From 5 to 15 years of age, normally developing children show an increase in ability to focus on and to recall relevant information, with a large increment in ability occurring at ages 12 and 13. They also show no increase, or very little increase over the 5- to 15-year age span, in learning and recall of incidental information. Children apparently are learning to focus their energies on relevant information and to disregard irrelevant information, resulting in greater learning and retention of more important information, and less learning of and retention of the other information.

Other studies implicate attention in learning disabilities, and sometimes in mental retardation. Krupski (1980) found learning-disabled and mentally retarded children deficient on high-demand voluntary attention tasks, but not on short-term, involuntary attention tasks. Mentally retarded children were also more distracted, only when observed working in classrooms, than were normal children (Krupski, 1979). Outside the classroom the mentally retarded children sustained attention well. These findings imply that because voluntary, sustained attention, especially as it occurs in high-demand academic settings, is deficient in these learners, attention-training programs might ameliorate some of these learning difficulties.

The same hope has emerged from research on hyperkinetic behavior problems among children, which recently were classified by the American Psychiatric Association as attentional deficit disorders. The research indicates that hyperkinetic activity frequently responds well to stimulant drugs.

The apparent paradox of this finding is understandable, if hyperactivity involves a deficit in attention. Hyperkinetic children are often no more highly aroused than other children, nor does a stimulant drug usually reduce their arousal. Instead hyperkinetic children have a relatively flat gradient of attention, and are unable to inhibit responses well to task-relevant but distracting stimulation, When they function well, the stimulant drugs steepen this gradient, and improve the children's selective attention (Conners, 1976).

From the teacher's perspective, the hyperkinetic children given stimulant drugs seem to be quieter and less active. More probably, the children are more cognitively active in an organized, task-relevant way. Their former disorganized, task-irrelevant overt behavior subsides, which leads to the teacher's observation that their activity is reduced. Instead, their activity level probably remains high, and has probably been directed into more productive and coherent thought processes. However, the drugs are far from ideal ways to facilitate learning. In addition to the obvious and serious physical problems of drug use, hyperactive children given stimulants can come to feel that they are helpless to control their behavior, and that their learning is due to a drug, not to their effort or ability.

Recent research on attention offers a useful alternative treatment. If hyperactivity is a problem of voluntary attention, then it is possible that the teaching of cognitive strategies for consciously controlling attention might enable some children to increase attention and to enhance learning, without the physical and attributional complications that can occur with stimulant drugs (Meichenbaum & Goodman. 1971).

To explore these possibilities several attentional cognitive training programs have been developed and tested with hyperactive and normal children. Douglas, Parry, Martin, and Garson (1976) taught 7- and 8-year-old hyperactive children to use self-talk to control their attention. After 3 months of training, their attention improved, as did their scores on the Matching Familiar Figures Test (a measure of ability to analyze details in pictures), tests of planning, and some tests of oral and listening comprehension, although reading was not taught in this program. Apparently the instruction generalized beyond the training tasks to influence ability to learn to read in the classroom.

Camp (1980), using techniques derived from Donald Meichenbaum's "stop, look, and listen" strategy, taught impulsive elementary school boys a four-step procedure to follow. Ask yourself (a) what problem you face, (b) how you will solve it (c) whether you are following your plan, and (d) how well you did with the problem. After 30 teaching sessions, the children showed gains in reading, IQ, and social behavior, which transferred to learning in the classroom.

These results show how the study of student thought processes can provide a new understanding of a learning disability that leads to cognitive training programs that might reduce or, in some cases, replace the use of stimulant drugs. This use of cognitive training programs has practical utility because the widespread use of stimulant drugs to facilitate learning is highly questionable and raises serious issues regarding its effects on children.

Using similar techniques, but with poor readers who were not hyperactive, Malamuth (1979) improved sustained attention. Reading scores also improved.

Other studies by other researchers have shown little or no

effect due to strategy training programs, especially short-term programs. Generalization of training programs is also a problem, although the cognitive strategy programs, compared with behavioristic or drug programs, obtain the greatest transfer to classroom learning (Keogh & Glover, 1980). Even with these problems and caveats, these results suggest new procedures, directed at changing student thoughts, that promise practical ways to ameliorate some difficult and important learning problems. For further discussion of the educational applications of these types of cognitive training programs see Meichenbaum and Asarnow (1978).

In the earlier section on student perceptions we found that attention, as a cognitive process, offered a useful concept for explaining how time to learn leads to student achievement. Measures of attention, especially student reports of attention, correlated with achievement more highly than did measures of children's time-to-learn or observers' records of their time-on-task.

In this latter section on attention we again saw the promise and the complications that attentional constructs bring to the problem of relating teaching to achievement. From these complementary lines of cognitive research, attention, as a student thought process, deserves further study, and attentional training programs deserve further development and application. With the construct of attention inserted as a mediator between teaching and achievement our ability to predict learning from instruction increases, as does our ability to understand some of the effects of teaching upon classroom achievement and upon some learning disorders.

As a result of the increased understanding of these learning mechanisms in and out of the classroom, we can sometimes design teaching procedures, such as teachers' questions and learners' use of objectives, and remedial cognitive training programs, such as attentional programs for hyperkinetic learners of school tasks. These teaching procedures and cognitive training strategies are simple to use, inexpensive, usually easily understood by teachers, and are teachable in the classroom. Their successful application however, involves sustained, lengthy, and repeated practice in a variety of contexts that will facilitate transfer to the learning of reading, mathematics, and other subjects taught in school.

Motivation

One of the most frequently studied and useful thought processes involved in learning from teaching is motivation, the process of initiating, sustaining, and directing activity. In modern times research on motivation in teaching has focused on topics such as reinforcement, need for achievement, intrinsic and extrinsic motivation, locus of control, and most recently, attribution. As an example of how recent research on students' motivational thought processes can enhance understanding of learning from teaching we will discuss some of the recent findings and theories emerging from research on student attribution, which is the study of students' perception of the causes of their successes and failures as learners. From this research have come new explanations for the effectiveness of several concepts, such as reinforcement, teacher praise and blame, and new instructional programs in attributional retraining and in self-management skills.

Children's concepts of the causes of their successes and failures develop from a relatively undifferentiated state to a more analytic conception of the relations among ability, effort, and achievement. At about 6 years of age many children do not separate ability, effort, and achievement (Nicholls, 1978). They equate effort to intelligence, and success to smart people who work hard. At about 7 to 8 years of age they distinguish these three concepts form one another, and causally relate effort, but not ability, to achievement. At about ages 9 to 11 years, ability also becomes a cause of achievement, but they still believe that people who work hard are also intelligent or able individuals. Beginning about age 11, children realize that effort and ability are relatively independent of each other, and are causally related to achievement. This developmental progression implies that training programs designed to teach children to ascribe success and failure to effort rather than to ability are likely to be effective primarily with children who are old enough to differentiate these concepts from one another, and who realize that each of them can independently influence achievement.

Children also develop in their concept of locus of control, their belief that events they experience are under their own or internal control, rather than under the control of other people or forces outside themselves, that is, under external control. From Jean Piaget's research on causal reasoning (e.g., Piaget &

Inhelder, 1975) young children often overestimate their ability to control events, including the weather and the movements of the sun and other stars.

On the other hand, researchers, such as Lefcourt (1976; 2nd ed.,1982), predict that internality, at least when measured as perceived competence, increases with age among children. Some measures of locus of control, such as Nowicki-Strickland Internal-External Control Scale, assume a developmental increase in internality from elementary school-age children through senior high school.

The observed development in children's locus of control depends on the type of test items used to measure it. Weisz and Stipek (1982) found that "agree-disagree" scales generally found internality to increase with age, while "choice-of-attribution" scales usually show no developmental increment in internality. They explained these results by hypothesizing that perceived competence, the ability to perform activities effectively, increases with age, but perceived contingency, the perception of the relation between one's actions, including competently performed acts, and observed outcomes, such as changes in other people's behavior, or the movements of stars, declines. The two types of scales measuring locus of control seem to involve both of these two dimensions of locus of control.

These developmental findings have been presented here because they provide a context for understanding the research on attribution and its implications and limitations for understanding learning in schools, and for designing attribution change programs and self-management instructional programs.

From a background of research on need achievement and locus of control, studies and models of attribution have tried to explicate the perceived causes, the "why," or the explanations learners construct to explain their past behavior and to motivate their future behavior. Weiner (1979, 1983), who believes that locus of control consists of two dimensions, causality and controllability, separates them from each other and adds a third dimension, stability, to his model of attributional processes. Locus of causality can be either internal or external in Weiner's system. Controllability can be either uncontrollable or controllable; and stability can be either stable or unstable.

Within this three-dimensional system, the perceived causes most often researched in educational contexts are (a) ability, a stable, internal, and uncontrollable cause; (b) effort (actually immediate effort), an unstable, internal, and controllable cause; (c) luck, an unstable, external, and uncontrollable cause; and (d) task difficulty, a stable, external, and uncontrollable cause.

One hypothesis emerging from this and related models of attributional processes is that students will be highly motivated to continue to learn when they attribute success or failure to their effort, or lack of it, rather than to forces over which they have little or no control, such as their ability, luck, or other people. Although there are complications with this straightforward and useful idea, a large number of empirical studies support it and its underlying attributional model. We discuss these studies next, focusing on attributional processes involving control and locus of causality.

As I mentioned earlier in this chapter, Coleman, et al. (1966) found that, among many minority groups of children in schools, one of the most powerful variables for explaining differences in achievement was the students' perceived lack of control over events in school, although they felt they had the ability to succeed. In agreement with that finding, Nowicki and Strickland (1973) found that school achievement correlated more highly with measures of locus of control than it did with measures of intelligence. Reid and Croucher (1980) found the same type of result, using a different test of locus of control, the Crandall Intellectual Achievement Responsibility Questionaire.

At the college level, measures of locus of control usually do not predict achievement well, although Nord, Connelly, and Diagnault (1974) found that Rotter's I–E scale, a measure of locus of control, did correlate with achievement in a complementary way to a measure of ability, an admissions test for entry into a business school. Ability and locus of control seemed to explain relatively separate or nonoverlapping portions of the variance in academic achievement. From these and other studies (see Bar-Tal, 1978, for further comment on relations between attributions and school achievement), it is clear that motivational thought processes can differentiate high and low achievers in schools and can predict learning from teaching.

Beyond their utility for predicting school achievement, motivational variables suggest how teaching processes influence the student thought processes that mediate achievement. These explanations represent attribution theory's major contribution, and lead to recently developed attributional retraining programs and self-management instructional materials, which we discuss next.

As an example of the type of explanation of teaching processes offered by attribution theory, consider how reinforcement might function to enhance learning. Attribution theory suggests that success is not enough to increase learning and achievement, which do not occur automatically or without mediation by students' thoughts. Reinforcement attributed by students to easy tasks, luck, ability, and even to excellent teachers, all internal or external factors over which the students have little control, will not increase persistence or motivation. The reason is that the students cannot or do not see that their effort contributed to the success. The theory also explains how contingent reinforcement, and sometimes teacher praise, functions to increase achievement by conveying to students that their effort produced the learning in school. Stated differently, success is not enough by itself. It must be perceived to be caused, at least in substantial part, by student effort, or other student processes under self-control and relevant to influencing learning outcomes. The theory further implies that effort invested in learning is not itself sufficient for enhancing motivation to learn. The students must perceive the causal relation between their effort and their success or failure in school.

These concepts have been studied in several educational contexts. Wang and Stiles (1976) found that students who believe their effort influences their achievement are more likely to learn than are students who believe that learning depends on teachers or other people (see also Andrews & Debus, 1978).

Dweck (1975) and Dweck, Davidson, Nelson, and Enna (1978) studied learned helplessness. Learned helplessness occurs when students feel that they cannot overcome failure. In the former study (Dweck, 1975), a group of children with learned helplessness were taught to take responsibility for their failures in school and to attribute them to lack of sufficient effort rather than to lack of ability. Another group of children with learned helplessness were given a success-only training program. The children given the attribution retraining program improved, or at least maintained, their academic performance, while the success-only group of children continued to decline in school achievement. One implication of this finding is that behavior modification programs providing only success experiences may be insufficient for teaching children to attribute their successes to their own effort and to take responsibility for their learning.

In the second experiment, Dweck et al. (1978) studied differences in boys and girls in learned helplessness. Girls show learned helplessness more often than do boys. Perhaps because of the different feedback from teachers, girls attribute failure to lack of ability, while boys tend more often to attribute failure to lack of effort. Teachers frequently criticize boys in elementary school for nonintellectual acts, and for lack of effort, while girls are criticized almost exclusively for intellectual activities. Because of the differential criticism, boys may have more readily attributed failure to lack of effort and girls may have more readily attributed it to lack of ability.

In this study, Dweck et al. treated both boys and girls to either a teacher–boy or a teacher–girl work-related criticism. Both boys and girls who received the teacher–girl treatment came to believe that lack of ability was the cause of failure in class. (However, Heller and Parsons, 1981, did not replicate these findings.)

From Dweck's data it is possible that teachers influence learning and achievement by the way they communicate attributions differently to some boys and girls. Again, the effects of success, praise, and reinforcement depend upon the interpretations students place upon them, and upon the way they perceive them to reflect upon their performance, their ability, and their effort.

deCharms (1972) taught teachers and students, over a 2-year training program, to perceive themselves as "origins," that is, as people who can control the outcomes of teaching and can take responsibility for teaching and learning, rather than as "pawns," that is, as people who cannot control learning and teaching and cannot take responsibility for them. The origin training program increased teacher and student motivation, language skills, and arithmetic achievement. Reading was least enhanced. The program worked better with boys than with girls. The control group continued to decline in percentile rank, as it had prior to the beginning of the 2-year study, while the origin training students gained 1 year per year of enrollment in school.

In addition to these attributional retraining programs, attribution theory has led to the development of instructional programs in self-management skills, and tests of self-responsibility for learning (Wang & Stiles, 1976; Wang, 1983). These instructional programs teach students not only to exercise control and responsibility over their learning, but to set realistic goals, to manage time available to learn, and to organize information to be learned. Proficiency at these self-management skills builds a student's sense of control and responsibility and facilitates the percentage of tasks successfully completed.

From a somewhat different perspective, applying concepts about self-efficacy as well as attribution retraining, Barbara McCombs (1982, 1983) developed an extensive motivational skills training program designed to teach adult students in the military services to take responsibility for learning and to exert self-control over their strategies for acquiring information from teachers. In addition to the motivational training lessons, the program included training in metacognitive skills, including planning, monitoring and assessment, and cognitive skills such as attention, comprehension, and memory. The motivational training program increased knowledge acquisition in the technical training course, reduced absenteeism, and, by observer ratings, increased motivation to learn, when compared with a comparable control group of students.

From this sample of research on motivation, there are data to indicate that the study of student thought processes leads to new ways to predict and to understand achievement from teaching. The theory and the research also lead to useful training programs that change the ways students think about their role and responsibility in learning from teaching. These implications have already been discussed in this section. Instead of reviewing that discussion, a few comments will be provided to elaborate their meaning and their limitations.

First, the idea of student responsibility for learning does not imply a lessened teacher responsibility for teaching, as is often inappropriately inferred from these data. Rather, each participant, teacher and learner, has a distinct responsibility for achievement. Good teaching is not enough for high achievement. Good learning, the active mental contribution of the learner, is a necessary component in this model for achievement to occur. Teaching exerts its influence on achievement through students' motivational processes, which can be controlled directly by the student as well as by the teacher or other people and factors.

Second, attribution change programs that depend upon changing ability or luck for effort attributions seem to assume that learners are capable of distinguishing effort, ability, and achievement from one another. Young children in primary school often do not make these distinctions, and are not likely to learn well from attribution retraining programs that involve knowledge of the different meanings of these terms or of the implications of seeing relations develop beween effort and achievement.

Third, change to effort attributions through retraining programs or teachers' use of praise and feedback should be followed by success in school, if students are to learn that effort leads to success. One implication of this finding is that teachers must choose difficulty levels appropriately to allow effort to lead to success in schools.

Last of all, attributions themselves may involve other cognitive or affective thought processes that will lead to improved understanding of the mediation of student achievement. Attribution of success to effort may lead to enhanced self-efficacy or self-control which enhances learning. Weiner (1983) has begun to study these processes.

In another context, patients' perceived control over the onset and cause of the pain reduces its intensity (Thompson, 1981). The perceived control changes the experiences of pain, perhaps by changing attributions and by increasing a sense of self-control of efficacy. Although it does not involve students in classrooms, the finding again shows the utility of studying thought processes of people learning to solve problems.

The study of motivation has produced changes in the ways we think about student responsibility for learning, teachers' feedback, praise, reinforcement, and the students' interpretation of the causes of success and failure in school.

For the future, research in motivation should study how attribution to cognitive strategies, rather than ability or effort, might influence learning and achievement. Strategy attribution might be effective with unsuccessful but hardworking students for whom training in effort attributions would make little sense.

Learning and Memory

From the recent laboratory and classroom study of learning and knowledge acquisition we have developed a new understanding of the cognitive processes that mediate learning from teaching. From this recent research we have also developed a few useful and practical instructional methods and programs that facilitate factual learning, learning with understanding, and the direct teaching of learning strategies and metacognitive processes.

These teaching procedures and instructional programs derive from principles that emphasize the cognitive processes involved in learning and comprehension. People learn not only by associating their actions to consequences, by reinforced practice, but also by observing others, by imitating them, by generating images, inferences, plans, and analogies, by listening to a teacher, and by reading, often without practice, reward, or feedback from others.

Two of these newly studied cognitive principles of learning and memory are as old as ideas common in ancient Greece and Rome. The first principle is that one learns and remembers information by associating ideas to one another. Aristotle's (reprinted, 1964) model of memory was based on the principle of associating ideas in order, one to another, and in storing these ideas as images in long-term memory, which one could retrieve by recalling one of them; and that would lead successively to each subsequent idea in the sequence. In the paragraphs below, we will see that the Aristotelian model underlies some of the modern-day research on the facilitation of learning and remembering factual information in schools, such as the capitals of states.

A second principle of ancient origin is that learning and memory increase when learners relate information to their knowledge store and to their experience. In ancient Greece and Rome, when rhetoric was still the art of public speaking, teachers, students, lawyers, and statesmen were regularly taught to form relations between familiar objects in their homes or offices and the points they wished to make in their talks or presentations.

In modern times this same principle is again used to facilitate memory. In addition, a modification of it leads to a new way to enhance comprehension through teaching learners to relate new information to their organized knowledge, or to accommodate their knowledge to the new information. In either case, I maintain in my model of generative learning (Wittrock, 1974a, 1978, 1981) that comprehension involves learners in the generation of relations between or among the parts — the words, sentences, and ideas, for example, in the materials they are learning. Learning with understanding includes also the generation of relations between previously acquired knowledge and the information to be learned, and between or among the parts — the words, sentences and ideas, for example, in the material to be comprehended. Both learning with understanding and factual or other learning that need not lead to understanding involve learner generation of relations. However, the meaningful nature of the relations differs because of the way the information relates to other information, to the learner's experience, and the learner's organized knowledge.

One frequently studied ancient method of facilitating learning and memory, especially of factual rather than conceptual materials, involves students in the use of imagery, such as text with high-imagery words, pictures or teacher-given instructions for students to construct their own images. Prior to age 8 or 9 years, pictures and high-imagery words, but not student-generated images, facilitate learning and memory (Levin, 1981). Wittrock and Goldberg (1975) found that high imagery words facilitate memory among elementary school children and college students. Prior to ages 8 or 9, children seem to have a production deficiency; that is, they can use images given to them by others, but they cannot, upon request, construct them to facilitate their own learning and memory.

An extensive number of studies has shown the facilitating effect of imagery, especially pictures, on learning and memory. Levin, Shriberg, Miller, McCormick, and Levin (1980) found that fourth and fifth graders who had been taught an imagery mnemonic system for remembering the capitals of the states in the United States remembered considerably more of them than did a comparable group given an equal amount of time to learn them using whatever procedures they chose. In a follow-up study, Levin, Berry, Miller, and Bartell (1982, p. 386) found that for their imagery mnemonic to function properly the students must be familiar with the names of capitals. Their mnemonic is based on a "keyword" associated with the name of each capital, and an interactive image that relates the state and the keyword. Their model applies the ancient principle of associating something new with something known or familiar. In addition, they use interactive pictures, another technique taught by teachers of rhetoric in ancient Rome (Yates, 1966) to facilitate memory.

Apparently the facilitation occurs by juxtaposing the familar element, which becomes the retrieval cue, such as a piece of furniture in one's home, with the unfamiliar element, such as the first point to be delivered in the orator's speech.

In Levin's studies, the state is the familiar retrieval cue, which leads to the interactive picture, which leads to the keyword, which leads to the name of the capital, the unfamiliar word. Levin adds another element to the sequence, the keyword, but the process is basically the ancient technique.

Sweeny and Bellezza (1982) used the keyword imagery mnemonic to teach college students the definitions of unfamiliar and abstract words. Compared with a group of students who learned the same word definitions in sentences with the keyword imagery technique, recall was sizeably increased, from 23% to 35%.

With Spanish vocabulary words, Raugh and Atkinson (1975) increased college students' retention from 28% to 88% by use of the keyword imagery mnemonic. These same authors also increased retention of Russian vocabulary words from 46% to 72%, again using the keyword imagery mnemonic. Bull and Wittrock (1973) found that sixth graders remembered word definitions better when they drew their own pictures of them, rather than when a comparable group of students, given equal time to learn, memorized the dictionary definitions. Levin, Shriberg, and Berry (1983) compared three types of illustrations to facilitate learning and memory of fictitious towns: (a) separate illustrations; (b) thematic illustrations, which integrated the separate illustrations into one picture; and (c) thematic or organized illustrations supplemented with cues associated by keywords to the town's name. The organized picture supplemented with keywords produced the greatest facilitation of memory of the four characteristics or attributes, followed by the organized picture, both of which were considerably higher than the separate pictures and a control condition.

Although they have not often been used to facilitate comprehension, imagery techniques, which involve spatial juxtaposition of ideas and objects, have potential value for facilitating understanding. We saw one beginning of interest developing in research in this area with the study (Levin et al., 1983) on remembering the organization of a passage that described cities and their characteristics. See Levin (1981, in press) for further discussions of imagery and its educational implications. See

Pressley, Levin, and Delaney (1982) for a review of research on the keyword method. Whether they function to increase comprehension, imagery techniques clearly have been shown to facilitate factual learning in classroom contexts, using procedures reminiscent of ancient methods. See Yates (1966) for a discussion of the memory principles that underlie the teaching functions of imagery in medieval religious art and architecture.

Verbal student thought processes have also been shown to facilitate memory of words, sometimes with dramatic gains. Bower and Clark (1969) increased college students' retention of a list of words from about 14 % to about 94 % by teaching them to construct simple stories from the words, keeping the words in the stories in the same order they appeared in the list. Wittrock and Carter (1975) asked college students to generate associations among hierarchically related words. Whether the words were conceptually related or only randomly ordered, the construction of relations among them sizeably increased their learning and retention.

Although many of these studies were conducted in classroom settings, we must still be cautious in applying their findings to classroom teaching because written materials or other instructional processes were often used instead of teachers.

The research on imagery and verbal processes indicates that instruction facilitates memory of factual material by either giving the learners, or asking them to generate, interactive associations among the new ideas, words, .or other information they are to learn and to remember, and between these ideas and their familiar experience. When the order of the ideas or words is important, the generated associations, such as stories, should maintain the serial order of the information to be remembered. Images and verbal generations facilitate memory of ideas and information primarily by the representation they provide of the relations among the parts or elements of a written passage, and the relations they show between the passage and one's experience. With imagery mnemonics and verbal elaborations, the generated relation is between something new and something old, something familiar.

Comprehension and Knowledge Acquisition

With at least one important difference, the teaching of comprehension and knowledge also involves the generation of relations among the elements of the information, for example, the words, sentences, and paragraphs of a text, and between the information and the learners' knowledge bases, as well as their experience (Wittrock, 1974a,b; 1983). According to my model of generative learning (Wittrock, 1981) comprehension is, essentially, the generation of a structural or conceptually ordered representation of the relations among the parts of the information to be learned, and between this information or these ideas and one's knowledge base and experience. Stated somewhat differently, the imagery mnemonics called "artificial" memory by ancient scholars, which involved learners' forming arbitrary associations between familiar objects or locations in one's home or office and information to be remembered, were adequate for facilitating memory, but not necessarily for facilitating comprehension of the points to be remembered. The reason is that the associations did not involve generating conceptual relations between the learner's knowledge and the information, nor the individual ideas or points to be remembered. With both comprehension and memory, the previously acquired information, knowledge, and experience are critical in their influence. To facilitate comprehension and knowledge acquisition, a teacher must build, or rather lead the learner to build, the cognitive relations we have discussed.

A wide variety of procedures for teaching learners to construct relations between their knowledge and experience and the information or concepts to be learned, and among the concepts to be learned, has been developed and studied empirically. One of the procedures asks students to generate relations between the text they are reading and their experience and knowledge.

Using elementary school teachers with students individually assigned at random to their classes, Linden and Wittrock (1981) taught fourth graders to generate verbal and spatial relations between the text and their knowledge and experience, as they read stories in their customarily used reading books. With time held constant across all groups, the children in the two experimental groups, who generated the relations between the text and their knowledge, substantially and statistically increased their reading comprehension, to means of 31.2 and 28.6 from a mean of 17.7 for the control group, who read the stories without instructions to generate relations. All three groups were taught by the senior author, who is a trained and experienced elementary school reading teacher. Another control group, taught by the students' regular fourth grade reading teacher, allowed to teach in any manner she chose, produced a mean of 21.6 well below (p < .01) the mean achievement of the experimental groups.

In a study using intact groups of learners and their regular classroom teachers, Au (1977) taught Hawaiian primary school children, who usually achieved two standard deviations below the mean score in reading, to relate their experiences to the Hawaiian stories read to them by their reading teacher. The primary school children stated in their own words several events in their lives that related to the stories. After one year of instruction, which probably involved other differences in instructional procedures as well, the experimental group scored at the 69th percentile of the Gates–MacGinite Reading Test, while the three control groups of first graders scored at the 8th, 21st, and 27th percentiles. Lesser but still large gains were also shown for second and third graders. See Tharp (1982) for a description of the instructional program used by Au. Pichert and Anderson (1977) asked college students to read a story about a house from the perspective of either a homebuyer or a burglar. The information the students learned and remembered depended upon the perspective they adopted. Dooling and Christiaansen (1977) told one group of college students that the story they were reading was about a familiar famous person, such as Helen Keller. The students' knowledge about the famous person led them to make inferences about the story that led to errors later, because the story was not actually about the famous person.

Familiar words and stories can also facilitate comprehension of new material, by enabling learners to generate relations between their knowledge base and the text they read. Wittrock, Marks, and Doctorow (1975) gave sixth graders a familiar story in which an undefined and unfamiliar vocabulary word was inserted into each sentence. The familiar context sizeably increased the understanding of the meaning of the vocabulary words, without defining them. In another experiment (Marks, Doctorow, & Wittrock, 1974) the substitution of one familiar word for an unfamiliar word in each sentence of a story enabled sixth graders to increase by 50% their comprehension of the texts they read. In each of these two studies, familiar ideas, either stories or words, enhanced the comprehension of unfamiliar material. These effects occurred across all different stories, tests, and student ability levels involved in the studies.

Mackenzie and White (1982) derived predictions from Wittrock's model of generative learning. They compared the effects upon ninth graders' learning induced by their actively relating the geography to concrete experiences provided by fieldwork, by active student generation of information, and by actively linking events with principles in geography. The generative, active learning group retained 90%, the passive learning group 58%, and a control group, 51% of the information they were taught.

Generating relations among the parts of the text — the sentences and the paragraphs, for example — by constructing summaries and headings, or by underlining main ideas, also facilitates comprehension and memory. Doctorow, Wittrock, and Marks (1978) gave 400 sixth graders a story to read from a commercially published reading series and asked them to generate a summary sentence for each paragraph they read, either with or without using the inserted paragraph headings. Compared with control groups given the same stories, and the same amount of time to learn, the generation of summaries, especially with use of the inserted headings, doubled comprehension. This result occurred across the two ability levels, stories, and tests used in the experiments.

Paris, Lindauer, and Cox (1977) taught 7- and 8-year-old children to construct stories and inferences about sentences they read. The construction of stories facilitated comprehension and memory of the sentences. Dee-Lucas and Di Vesta (1980) gave or had college students generate topic sentences, headings, related sentences, and unrelated sentences as they read a passage on minerals. The comprehension of the organization of the passage was facilitated most by the student generation of topic sentences. The constuction of sentences irrelevant to learning the organization of the passage, that is the so-called related sentences, reduced comprehension of the structure of the passage. Generation of topic sentences also reduced recall of factual information. It seems that generations that focus on comprehension of the organization of the passage facilitate its understanding, and reduce learning of its details. Generation of irrelevant or distracting materials reduces learning by the greatest amount, compared with teacher-given equivalents. Generation seems to be a powerful variable in these studies of verbal processes, provided the students have the age and the experience needed to perform it.

Rickards and August (1975) report a related finding with underlining of words in text, either by a teacher or by the learners. The highest learning occurred when learners underlined words they chose or words of high structural importance; while the lowest learning occurred when the learners were made to underline words of low structural importance, which was lower than that of a group that read the passage without instructions to underline words. Teacher-underlined words in the text produced results between the gains and decrements shown by the student-generated underlinings.

Again the results show a pattern that indicates the importance of actively involving students in the generation of relations among the parts of the text, when one wants to facilitate comprehension of it. Teacher-provided structure of the passage also facilitates comprehension, but not as much as does student-generated structure. Because of the power of this variable, it also produces the greatest reduction in comprehension when it is directed to irrelevant, and perhaps also to incorrect, generations of the structure of a passage. When it is done poorly, such as by students who have inadequate knowledge and ability, it can also be expected to reduce comprehension.

For these reasons the study of the students' knowledge base and ability to use learning strategies has received considerable attention recently. Pearson, Hansen, and Gordon (1979) found that second grade readers' inferential comprehension, but not factual information, of a passage about spiders depended upon their knowledge of spiders. Larkin (1981) found a difference in strategies of solving physics problems existing between experts and beginners. Chi, Glaser, and Rees (1981) found that these strategy differences involve the beginners' deficiencies in their knowledge about physics, rather than in their problem-solving strategies. The experts represent the problems more in terms of their principles of physics, while the beginners stress the surface or literal characteristics of the problem.

Roger Osborne studies the models children used to comprehend basic concepts in physical science (Osborne, 1981; Osborne & Wittrock, 1983). In research in New Zealand, Great Britain, and the United States he finds that elementary school children have basic models of scientific phenomena, such as of current flow between a battery and a light bulb connected in a simple direct current circuit, that often differ from the physicists' model of the same events. In these three countries, some children think that the electric current flows only in one half of the circuit, from the battery to the light bulb, for instance. They believe that the other wire, from the bulb to the battery, is for safety, for leakage of current. Another group of students thinks the current flows in two directions, one current from each side of the battery through its wire to the light bulb. They also think that the meeting of these opposing currents causes the light to glow. A third group of students perceives the current flow essentially as the physicists do, that it goes in one direction equal in amplitude throughout the circuit.

When children with the first two of these three models are shown data with ammeters that prove that their model is incorrect, they do not usually change their perception. Instead they often believe that outside the classroom, at home, for example, current flows the way they state that it does. Only in the classroom does current flow as the teacher thinks it does.

Children's reactions to teachers' attempts to change their models by showing them a dissonance between their belief and reality show the difficulty of teaching new theories and models. The students sometimes do not perceive a dissonance, as the teachers anticipated. The children finesse the problem by maintaining a sharp distinction between the perceived artificial school environment and the so-called real environment at home.

One implication of this finding is that teachers cannot plan on teaching only the difference between students' perceptions and scientists' models of scientific phenomena. The teaching problem involves relearning, or accommodating, students' theories and models. The first part of this teaching problem is learning the students' models. But changing these previously learned models involves more than knowing and recognizing them (Wittrock, 1963). This important area of research deserves further attention. For related findings in mathematics see Carpenter, Moser, and Romberg (1982).

In sum, from a variety of lines of research on comprehension, it seems that the generation of relations between knowledge and experience on the one hand, and the information to be learned, on the other hand, is an important mediator of teaching, as is the generation of relations among the elements of the materials to be learned. Both of these types of relations can be facilitated by either learner generation of them, when the student has the appropriate knowledge and ability, or by appropriate teacher-given structure and conceptual relations.

The teaching of new models or theories presents a complex problem that also involves the students' organized knowledge and experience. The research we have discussed implies that the learning of a new perspective or model involves the relearning or accommodation of a previously learned conception. Knowledge of that conception is a first step, but only that, toward designing instruction which must do more than simply teach the difference between students' beliefs and teachers' knowledge. The instruction should facilitate the construction of a new conceptual framework from an old preconception.

Learning Strategies and Metacognitive Processes

In this section we will discuss how students can be taught to be aware of and to control some of their thought processes, the topics studied in research on learning strategies and metacognitive processes.

However, learning strategies and metacognitive processes are the topics of a separate chapter by Weinstein and Mayer (this volume). For this reason they will not be discussed at length. Instead, to complete the theme of this chapter, I will briefly discuss some of the studies on the teaching of learning strategies and metacognitive processes to students. This discussion summarizes many of the findings already presented in this chapter.

For further discussion of learning strategies and metacognition, see Weinstein and Mayer (this volume), and Brown, Bransford, Ferrara, and Campione (1984). For further discussion of the development of metacognitive processes see Flavell (1979) and Mischel and Mischel (1983). For further discussion of research on cognitive strategies, see Pressley and Levin (1983a, 1983b).

Learning strategies, according to Weinstein and Mayer (this volume), are learners' actions and thoughts that occur during learning and that influence motivation and encoding, including acquisition, retention, and transfer.

Metacognition refers to the learners' knowledge about and control over their cognitive processes. Metacognition is a broad and loosely defined area that relates to many of the thought processes we have discussed in this chapter, which are being widely studied in education and in other fields. For example, Thompson (1981) reports that patients undergoing painful medical procedures reduced the intensity of pain they felt only when they were taught to use cognitive strategies, such as imaging situations incompatible with the pain, or thinking about the future benefits of surgery or childbirth. None of the other strategies, including behavioral and informational strategies, reduced the intensity of pain when it was actually occurring.

The teaching of learning strategies and metacognitive strategies has been found also to be effective in educational settings to facilitate attention, motivation, learning, memory, and comprehension, as well as to remediate some learning disabilities. Mischel and Baker (1975) used an attentional training program to increase delay of gratification among preschoolers, from 5 to 14 minutes, by teaching them to think of food as inedible objects. As previously discussed, Richard deCharms (1972) facilitated motivation in teachers and achievement in high school students by teaching them to think of themselves as origins rather than as pawns. Dweck (1975) enhanced motivation and achievement among "learned helpless" students by teaching them to attribute failure to lack of effort rather than to lack of ability. McCombs (1982) showed gains in learning among students in the military services as a result of a motivational training program that changed student attributions by emphasizing their responsibilities for learning through their own effort.

Learning and retention of subject matter taught in classrooms has been facilitated by learning strategy training using imagery (Levin et al., 1980, 1983; Levin, 1981), and verbal processes (Dansereau et al., 1979; C. Weinstein, 1982).

As mentioned earlier, the teaching of reading and reading comprehension has been frequently studied recently (Wittrock et al., 1975; Wittrock, 1974a). Some studies report sizeable gains in reaching comprehension due to the teaching of learning strategies or metacognitive processes (e.g., Brown et al., 1984; Doctorow et al., 1978; Linden & Wittrock, 1981; Wittrock, 1967, 1981).

Other school-taught subjects are also becoming involved in the identification and teaching of learning strategies and metacognitive processes. In the recent study of the cognitive processes of addition and subtraction, several authors (e.g., Carpenter & Moser, 1982) found that children usually begin to solve these problems by using their fingers and a "counting all with models" strategy. In this strategy they start counting in an addition problem, say 2 + 3, with the number 1, and continue using both hands to count both numbers, 2 and 3, until they reach the total. Later, they "count all without models," using the same counting technique, but not with their fingers as models. Later they "count on from the first or smaller number," and still later, they "count on from the larger number." From knowledge of this developmental progression of strategies, one could devise instruction to teach children more advanced strategies to use.

Brown and Vanlehn (1982) identified faulty strategies or "bugs" children use in subtraction problems. Knowledge of these strategies enables a teacher to understand the repeated errors children make and to provide instruction that goes beyond giving positive or negative feedback for each individual problem. The identification of the strategies also raises the possibility of teaching better strategies to facilitate subtraction.

As we saw earlier with Roger Osborne's research on children's models of science concepts, understanding children's thinking about science concepts is only the first part of designing instruction for the students. The teaching of new learning strategies to replace less effective ones poses unsolved problems.

In earlier sections of this chapter we also discussed the positive effects of Donald Meichenbaum's, Bonnie Camp's, and Virginia Douglas' metacognitive training programs for learning-disabled children. These programs enhanced student planning and self-control over learning. Each program showed transfer to learning in schools. In addition, we saw that similar self-management programs for children with reading disabilities (Malamuth, 1979) also facilitated achievement in school. In an issue of the *Journal of Topics in Learning and Learning Disabilities* "Metacognition and Learning Disabilities," (1982) the promise of instruction in metacognitive processes is discussed, including their utility for improving reading performance in school. See also Feuerstein's (1980) comprehensive cognitive training program for teaching children in school to change their thought processes and to increase achievement in reading and mathematics.

From this broad base of research on the teaching of metacognitive processes and learning strategies, the future for enhancing school achievement by use of "learning how to learn" techniques looks promising. Students can be taught learning strategies, in some instances at least, that sizeably enhance their learning. When students become aware of the processes they are using, and when they learn to control these cognitive processes, their transfer of them often increases (Brown et al., 1984).

For the future, we need research on the relation between the development of and the teaching of learning strategies and metacognitive processes. The development of learning strategies and metacognitive processes tends to follow the learner's development of relevant knowledge (Armbruster, Echols, & Brown, 1983). The teaching of these cognitive processes should involve a thorough knowledge of their development and an understanding of the students' knowledge base. With the understanding of these developmental processes and children's relevant knowledge base, it seems quite possible that instruction in learning strategies and metacognitive processes, including awareness and control of one's own learning, can facilitate achievement. It also seems possible that some of these learning strategies and metacognitive processes will generalize across different subject matters. Knowledge about learning how to learn may be useful in a variety of school-related areas, may apply across several subjects taught in school, and may be useful with different ability levels and with learning disorders.

Summary

We began this chapter with the distinctive perspective that underlies the recent research on students' thought processes. That perspective emphasizes how teaching influences achievement through student thought processes. Throughout the chapter, we discussed research on the student thought processes that represent a coherent set of cognitions centrally involved in mediating the effects of teaching. From the theory and research we reviewed, several implications for designing research on teaching and several findings relevant to understanding the effects of teaching upon student achievement were developed. Among these implications for the design of research was the finding that the study of student mediating processes provides a useful way to ask new questions about teaching, and to develop and to test hypotheses that explain, as well as predict, some of the effects of teaching.

Among the findings relevant to understanding the effects of

teaching upon student achievement were the following results and explanations. In the area of student perceptions and expectations, the research indicates that student belief that success in school is possible is one of the most important factors related to school achievement. In addition, research on student perceptions and expectations finds that the teacher expectation effect, the self-fulfilling prophecy, often depends upon the individual student's ability to perceive the teacher's expectation and differential treatment of students in the classroom. The implication is that studying teacher behavior as it relates to student thought processes as mediators of achievement provides a productive way to understand results sometimes difficult to explain by correlating teacher behavior or teaching processes directly to student achievement. The research also indicates that even in intact classrooms, the individual student, or the teacher–student dyad, is the appropriate unit of statistical analysis. The reason is that student expectations differ among students in the same class given the same treatment by teachers. The students do not always sense the treatment, differential or similar, they are given by their teachers.

In the study of attention, related findings also occur. Self-report measures of attention correlate more highly with student achievement than do measures of time-to-learn or time-on-task, which do not necessarily measure student thought processes. Consequently, it seems plausible to hypothesize that measures of time-to-learn or of time-on-task predict achievement insofar as they correlate with attention. and other thought processes that may not accurately be equated to observable time-on-task, or to time-to-learn. The implication of this finding for understanding teaching is that the students' proper use of the time, not only the time "on-task" or the time allocated by the teacher to learning, influences achievement.

In the study of student motivation, the learners' attributions about the causes of their success and failure influence their interest and persistence in learning in schools. Success in school enhances motivation primarily when the students attribute the results to their own effort, rather than to other people or factors outside their control. Rewards do not seem to strengthen learning or motivation automatically, nor even primarily in the student receiving them. Instead, the rewards seem to convey information about correct answers and teacher goals and desires to many attentive students who observe the teacher and the rewarded student.

In the study of learning and memory, as well as in comprehension and knowledge acquisition, it is again the learners' generation of meaning from the teaching that influences achievement. Learning and memory are facilitated when the learners construct images and verbal representations that relate old memories to new information, especially in organized or sequenced ways.

Comprehension and knowledge acquisition are facilitated when learners incorporate new information into familiar frameworks, or revise conceptual frameworks to accommodate new information that is incompatible with the preconceptions. From this research, teaching to facilitate learning and comprehension should focus on engaging the learner in constructing relations among the elements of the subjects to be learned, and between knowledge and experience, on the one hand, and the information or conceptualizations to be learned, on the other hand.

In the study of learning strategies and metacognitive processes the effects of students' awareness and control over these thought processes have been examined. These newly emerging findings, still tentative, indicate that with some subjects taught in school, such as reading, and with some learning disorders and hyperactivity, the teaching of learning strategies and metacognitive processes can facilitate achievement.

In sum, research on student processes revises the design of studies on teaching by including in them models and data about cognitive and affective processes that mediate the effects of teaching upon student achievement. Provided the mediators are parsimoniously used and carefully measured and quantified, they can facilitate understanding of the effects of teaching upon students.

In the studies reviewed in this chapter, the results indicate some of the value of student mediating processes for explaining the effects of teaching upon achievement, and for revising our understanding of how fundamentally important teaching variables and learning processes, including reward, teacher expectations, time-on-task, success in school, learning, and knowledge acquisition, function in schools. In each case, it is the learners' generation of meaning from the teaching that mediates the achievement.

REFERENCES

Amatora, M. (1952). Can elementary school children discriminate certain traits in their teachers? *Child Development, 23*, 75-80.

Ames, C. (1981). Competitive versus cooperative reward structures: The influence of individual and group performance factors on achievement attributions and affect. *American Educational Research Journal, 18*, 273-287.

Anderson, L. (1981). Short-term student responses to classroom instruction. *Elementary School Journal, 82*, 97-108.

Anderson, L., Evertson, C., & Brophy, J. (1979). An experimental study of effective teaching in first-grade reading groups. *Elementary School Journal 79*, 193-223.

Andre, T, (1979). Does answering higher-level questions while reading facilitate productive learning? *Review of Educational Research, 49*, 280-318.

Andrews, G. R., & Debus, R. L. (1978). Persistence and causal perception of failure: Modifying cognitive attributions. *Journal of Educational Psychology, 70*, 154-166.

Aristotle. (1964). On memory and recollection. In W. S. Hett (Trans.), *On the soul (De anima); Parva naturalia; and On breath* (Appendix). Cambridge, MA: Harvard University Press, Loeb Classical Library.

Armbruster, B. B., Echols, C. H., & Brown, A. L. (1983, April). *The role of metacognition in reading to learn: A developmental perspective* (Reading Education Rep. No. 40). Champaign: University of Illinois, Center for the Study of Reading.

Au, K. (1977, December). *Cognitive training and reading achievement.* Paper presented at the meeting of the Association for the Advancement of Behavior Therapy, Atlanta, GA.

Bar-Tal, D. (1978). Attributional analysis of achievement-related behavior. *Review of Educational Research, 48*, 259-271.

Beam, K. J., & Horvat, R. E. (1975). Differences among teachers' and students' perceptions of science classroom behaviors and actual classroom behaviors. *Science Education, 59*, 333-334.

Beck, W. R. (1967). Pupils' perceptions of teacher merit: A factor analysis of five postulated dimensions. *Journal of Educational Research, 61*, 127-128.

Blumenfeld, P. C., Hamilton, V. L., Bossert, S. T., Wessels, K., & Meece, J. (1983). Teacher talk and student thought: Socialization into the student role. In J. Levine & M. C. Wang (Eds.), *Teacher and student / perceptions: Implications for learning.* Hillsdale, NJ: Lawrence Erlbaum.

Boker, J. R. (1974). Immediate and delayed retention effects of interspersing questions in written instructional passages. *Journal of Educational Psychology, 66*, 96-98.

Bower, G. H., & Clark, M. C. (1969). Narrative stories as mediators for serial learning. *Psychonomic Science, 14*, 181-182.

Braun, C. (1976). Teacher-expectation: Sociopsychological dynamics. *Review of Educational Research, 46*, 185-213.

Brookover, W. B., Beady, C., Flood, P., Schweitzer, J., & Weisenbaker,

J. (1977). *Schools can make a difference.* East Lansing: Michigan State University, Center for Urban Affairs.

Brophy, J. E. (1981). Teacher praise: A functional analysis. *Review of Educational Research, 51,* 5–32.

Brophy, J. E. (1983). Research on the self-fulfilling prophecy and teacher expectations. *Journal of Educational Psychology, 75,* 631–661.

Brophy, J. E., & Evertson, C. (1976). *Learning from teaching: A developmental perspective.* Boston: Allyn & Bacon.

Brown, A. L., Bransford, J. D., Ferrara, R. A., & Campione, J. C. (1984). Learning, remembering, and understanding. In J. H. Flavell & M. Markman (Eds.), *Carmichael's manual of child psychology* (Vol. 3). New York: John Wiley, pp. 77–166.

Brown, J. S., & Vanlehn, K. (1982). Towards a generative theory of "bugs." In T. P. Carpenter, J. Moser, & T. Romberg (Eds.), *Addition and subtraction: A developmental perspective.* Hillsdale, NJ: Lawrence Erlbaum.

Bull, B. L., & Wittrock, M. C. (1973). Imagery in the learning of verbal definitions. *British Journal of Educational Psychology, 43,* 289–293.

Camp, B. W. (1980). Two psychoeducational treatment programs for young aggressive boys. In C. K. Whalen and B. Henker (Eds.), *Hyperactive children, the social ecology of identification and treatment.* New York: Academic Press, pp. 191–219.

Carpenter, T. P., & Moser, J. M. (1982). The development of addition and subtraction problem solving skills. In T. P. Carpenter, J. Moser, & T. Romberg (Eds.), *Addition and subtraction: A developmental perspective.* Hillsdale, NJ: Lawrence Erlbaum.

Carpenter, T. P., Moser, J., & Romberg T. (Eds.). (1982). *Addition and subtraction: A developmental perspective.* Hillsdale, NJ: Lawrence Erlbaum.

Chi, M. T. H., Glaser, R., & Rees, E. (1981). Expertise in problem-solving. In R. Sternberg (Ed.), *Advances in the psychology of human intelligence.* Hillsdale, NJ: Lawrence Erlbaum.

Coleman, J. S., Campbell, E. Q., Hobson, C. J., McPartland, J., Mood, A. A., Weinfeld, F. S., & York, R. L. (1966). *Equality of educational opportunity* (Report from the Office of Education). Washington, DC: U.S. Government Printing Office.

Conners, C. K. (1976). Learning disabilities and stimulant drugs in children: Theoretical implications. In R. M. Knights & D. J. Bakker (Eds.), *The neuropsychology of learning disorders.* Baltimore, MD: University Park Press.

Cooper, H. (1979). Pygmalion grows up: A model for teacher expectation communication and performance influence. *Review of Educational Research, 49,* 389–410.

Cooper, H. (1983). Communication of teacher expectations to students. In J. Levine & M. C. Wang (Eds.), *Teacher and student perceptions: Implications for learning.* Hillsdale, NJ: Lawrence Erlbaum.

Cooper, H. M., & Good, T. L. (1982). *Pygmalion grows up: Studies in the expectation communication process.* New York: Longmans.

Dansereau, D. F., Collins, K. W., McDonald, B. A., Holley, C. D.,

Garland, J., Diekhoff, G., & Evans, S. H. (1979). Development and evaluation of a learning strategy training program. *Journal of Educational Psychology, 71*, 64–73.

deCharms, R. (1972). Personal causation training in the schools. *Journal of Applied Psychology, 2*, 95–113.

Dee Lucas, D., & DiVesta, F. J. (1980). Learner generated organizational aids: Effects on learning from text. *Journal of Educational Psychology, 72*, 304–311.

Doctorow, M. J., Wittrock, M. C., & Marks, C. B. (1978). Generative processes in reading comprehension. *Journal of Educational Psychology, 70*, 109–118.

Dooling, D. J., & Christiaansen, R. E. (1977). Episodic and semantic aspects of memory for prose. *Journal of Experimental Psychology: Human Learning and Memory, 3*, 428–436.

Douglas, V. I., Parry, P., Martin, P., & Garson, C. (1976). Assessment of a cognitive training program for hyperactive children. *Journal of Abnormal Child Psychology, 4*, 389–410.

Doyle, W. (1977). Paradigms for research on teacher effectiveness. *Review of Research in Education, 5*, 163–198.

Doyle, W. (1980). *Student mediation responses in teaching effectiveness* (Final Report). Denton, Texas: North Texas State University.

Duchastel, P. Learning objectives and the organization of prose. *Journal of Educational Psychology*, 1979, *71*, 100–106.

Duell, O. K. Effect of type of objective, level of test questions, and the judged importance of tested materials upon posttest performance. *Journal of Educational Psychology*, 1974, *66*, 225–232.

Dweck, C. (1975). The role of expectations and attributions in the alleviation of learned helplessness. *Journal of Personality and Social Psychology, 31*, 674–685.

Dweck, C. S., Davidson, W., Nelson, S., & Enna, B. (1978). Sex differences in learned helplessness: 2. The contingencies of evaluative feedback in the classroom; 3. An experiment analysis. *Developmental Psychology, 14*, 268–276.

Evertson, C., Anderson, C., Anderson, L., & Brophy, J. (1980). Relationships between classroom behaviors and student outcomes in junior high mathematics and English classes. *American Educational Research Journal, 17*, 43–60.

Feuerstein, R. (1980). *Instrumental enrichment: An instructional program for cognitive modifiability*. Baltimore, Md.: University Park Press.

Filby, N., & Barnett, B. (1982). Student perceptions of better readers in elementary classrooms. *Elementary School Journal, 82*, 435–449.

Flavell, J. H. (1979). Metacognition and cognitive monitoring: A new area of cognitive-developmental inquiry. *American Psychologist, 34*, 906–911.

Heller, K. A., & Parsons, J. E. (1981). Sex differences in teachers' evaluative feedback and students' expectations for success in mathematics. *Child Development, 52*, 1015–1019.

Kaplan, R., & Simmons, F. G. (1974). Effects of instructional objectives used as orienting stimuli or as summary/review upon prose learning. *Journal of Educational Psychology*, 614–622.

Keogh, B. K., & Glover, A. T. (1980). The generalizability and durability of cognitive training effects. *Exceptional Education Quarterly, 1,* 75–82.

Koopman, C., & Newston, D. (1981). Level of analysis in the perception of ongoing instruction. *Journal of Educational Psychology, 73,* 212 223.

Krupski, A. (1979). Are retarded children more distractable? Observational analysis of retarded and nonretarded children's classroom behavior. *American Journal of Mental Deficiency, 84,* 1-10.

Krupski, A. (1980). Attention processes: Research, theory, and implications for special education. In B. Keogh (Ed.) *Advances in Special Education,* Vol. 1, JAI Press, pp. 101–140.

Larkin, J. H. (1981). Enriching formal knowledge: A model for learning to solve textbook physics problems. In J. Anderson (Ed.), *Cognitive skills and their acquisition.* Hillsdale, NJ: Lawrence Erlbaum.

Lefcourt, H. M. (1982). *Locus of control: Current trends in theory and research.* Hillsdale, NJ: Lawrence Erlbaum. (1st ed. publshed 1976)

Lepper, M. R. (1983). Extrinsic reward and intrinsic motivation. In J. Levine & M. C. Wang (Eds.), *Teacher and student perceptions: Implications for learning.* Hillsdale, NJ.: Lawrence Erlbaum.

Levin, J. R. (1981). On functions of pictures in prose. In F. J. Pirozzolo & M. C. Wittrock (Eds.), *Neuropsychological and cognitive processes of reading.* New York: Academic Press.

Levin, J. R. (in press). Educational applications of mnemonic pictures: Possibilities beyond your wildest imagination. In A. A. Sheikh (Ed.), *Imagery and the educational process.* Farmingdale, NY: Baywood Publishing.

Levin, J. R., Berry, J. K., Miller, G. E., & Bartell, N. P. (1982). More on how (and how not) to remember the states and their captials. *The Elementary School Journal, 82,* 371-388.

Levin, J. R., Shriberg, L. K., & Berry, J. K. (1983). A concrete strategy for remembering abstract prose. *American Educational Research Journal, 20,* 277-290.

Levin, J. R., Shriberg, L. K., Miller, G. E., McCormick, C. G., & Levin, B. B. (1980). The keyword method in the classroom: How to remember the states and their capitals. *Elementary School Journal, 80,* 185-191.

Linden, M., & Wittrock, M. C. (1981). The teaching of reading comprehension according to the model of generative learning. *Reading Research Quarterly, 17,* 44–57.

Livesley, W. J., & Bromley, D. (1973). *Person perception in childhood and adolescence.* London: John Wiley.

Mackenzie, A. W., & White, R. T. (1982). Fieldwork in geography and long-term memory structures. *American Educational Research Journal, 19,* 623-632.

Malamuth, S. (1979). Self-management training for children with reading problems: Effects on reading performance and sustained attention. *Cognitive Therapy and Research, 4,* 279-289.

Marks, C. B., Doctorow, M. J., & Wittrock, M. C. (1974). Word frequency and reading comprehension. *Journal of Educational Research, 67,* 259-262.

McCombs, B. L. (1982). Transitioning learning strategies research into practice: Focus on the student in technical training. *Journal of Instructional Development, 5*, 10-17.

McCombs, B. L. (1983, April). *Motivational skills training: Helping students to adapt by taking personal responsibility and positive self-control.* Paper presented at the annual meeting of the American Educational Research Association, Montreal.

Meichenbaum, D., & Asarnow, J. (1978). Cognitive-behavior modification and metacognitive development: Implications for the classroom. In P. Kendall & S. Hollen (Eds.), *Cognitive-behavioral interventions: Theory, research, and procedures.* New York: Academic Press.

Meichenbaum, D., & Goodman, J. (1971). Training impulsive children to talk to themselves: A means of developing self-control. *Journal of Abnormal Psychology, 77*, 115-126.

"Metacognition and Learning Disabilities" [special issue]. (1982). *Topics in Learning and Learning Disabilities, 2*(1), 1-107.

Mischel, H. N., & Mischel, W. (1983). The development of children's knowledge of self-control strategies. *Child Development, 54*, 603-619.

Mischel, W., & Baker, N. (1975). Cognitive appraisals and transformations in delay behavior. *Journal of Personality and Social Psychology, 31*, 254-261.

Morine-Dershimer, G. (1982). Pupil perceptions of teacher praise. *Elementary School Journal, 82*, 421-434.

Nicholls, J. G. (1978). The development of the concepts of effort and ability, perception of academic attainment, and the understanding that difficult tasks require more ability. *Developmental Psychology, 49*, 800-814.

Nicholls, J. G. (1979). Quality and equality in intellectual development. *American Psychologist, 34*, 1071-1084.

Nord, W. R., Connelly, F., & Diagnault, G. (1974). Laws of control and aptitude test scores as predictors of academic achievement. *Journal of Educational Psychology, 66*, 956-961.

Nowicki, S., Jr., & Strickland, B. R. (1973). A locus of control scale for children. *Journal of Consulting and Clinical Psychology, 40*, 148-154.

Osborne, R. (1981). Children's ideas about electric current. *New Zealand Science Teacher, 29*, 12-19.

Osborne, R. J., & Wittrock, M. C. (1983). Learning science: A generative process. *Science Education, 67*, 489-508.

Paris, S. G., Lindauer, B. K., & Cox, G. L. (1977). The development of inferential comprehension. *Child Development, 48*, 1728-1733.

Paton, S. M., Walberg, H. J., & Yeh, E. G. (1973). Ethnicity, environmental control, and academic self-concept in Chicago. *American Educational Research Journal, 10*, 85-99.

Pearson, P. D., Hansen, J., & Gordon, C. (1979, March). *The effect of background knowledge on young children's comprehension of explicit and implicit information* (Tech. Rep. NO. 116). Urbana: University of Illinois, Center for the Study of Reading.

Peterson, P. L., & Swing, S. R. (1982). Beyond time on task: Students' reports of their thought processes during direct instruction. *Elementary School Journal, 82*, 481-491.

Peterson, P. L., Swing, S. R., Braverman, M. T., & Buss, R. (1982). Students' aptitudes and their reports of cognitive processing during instruction. *Journal of Educational Psychology. 74*, 535-547.

Peterson, P. L., Swing, S. R., Stark, K. D., & Waas, G. A. (1983, April). *Students' reports of their cognitive processes and affective thoughts during classroom instruction.* Paper presented at the annual meeting of the American Educational Research Association, Montreal.

Piaget, J., & Inhelder, B. (1975). *The origin of the idea of chance in children.* New York: W.W. Norton.

Pichert, J. W., & Anderson, R. C. (1977). Taking different perspectives on a story. *Journal of Educational Psychology, 69*, 309-315.

Pressley, M., & Levin, J. (Eds.). (1983a). *Cognitive strategy research*: *Educational applications.* New York: Springer Verlag.

Pressley, M., & Levin, J. (Eds.). (1983b). *Cognitive strategy research*: *Psychological foundations.* New York: Springer Verlag.

Pressley, M., Levin, J., & Delaney, H. (1982). The mnemonic keyword method. *Review of Educational Research, 52*, 61-91.

Preston, M.S., Guthrie, J. T., & Childs, B. (1974). Visual evoked responses in normal and disabled readers. *Psychophysiology, 11*, 452-457.

Raugh, M. R., & Atkinson, R. C. (1975). A mnemonic method for learning a second-language vocabulary. *Journal of Educational Psychology, 67*, 1-16.

Reid, I., & Croucher, A. (1980). The Crandall Intellectual Achievement Responsibility Questionaire: A British validation study. *Educational and Psychological Measurement, 40*, 255-258.

Rickards, J. P., & August, G. J. (1975). Generative underlining strategies in prose recall. *Journal of Educational Psychology, 67*, 860-865.

Rickards, J. P., & Denner, P. R. (1978). Inserted questions as aids to reading text. *Instructional Science, 1*, 313-346.

Stayrook, N. G., Corno, L., & Winne, P. H. (1978). Path analyses relating student perceptions of teacher behavior to student achievement. *Journal of Teacher Education, 29*, 51-56.

Stipek, D. J. (1981). Children's perceptions of their own and their classmates' ability. *Journal of Educational Psychology, 73*, 404-410.

Stipek, D., & Hoffman, J. (1980). Children's achievement related expectancies as a function of academic performance histories and sex. *Journal of Educational Psychology, 72*, 861-865.

Sweeny, C. A., & Bellezza, F. S. (1982). Use of the keyword mnemonic in learning English vocabulary. *Human Learning, 1*, 155-163.

Thompson, S. C. (1981). Will it hurt less if I can control it? A complex answer to a simple question. *Psychological Bulletin, 90*, 89-101.

Tharp, R. (1982). The effective instruction of comprehension: Results and description of the Kamehameha Early Education Program. *Reading Research Quarterly, 17*, 503-527.

Wang, M. C. (1983). Development and consequences of students' sense of personal control. In J. Levine & M. C. Wang (Eds.), *Teacher and student perceptions: Implications for learning.* Hillsdale, NJ: Lawrence Erlbaum.

Wang, M. C., & Stiles, B. (1976). An investigation of children's concept of self-responsibility for their school learning. *American Educational Research Journal, 13,* 159-179.

Weiner, B. (1979). A theory of motivation for some classroom experiences. *Journal of Educational Psychology, 71,* 3-25.

Weiner, B. (1983). Speculations regarding the role of affect in achievement-change programs guided by attributional principles. In J. Levine & M. C. Wang (Eds.), *Teacher and student perceptions: Implications for learning.* Hillsdale, NJ: Lawrence Erlbaum.

Weinstein, C. E. (1982). Training students to use elaboration learning strategies. *Contemporary Educational Psychology, 7,* 301-311.

Weinstein, R. S. (1983). Student perceptions of schooling. *Elementary School Journal, 83,* 288-312.

Weinstein, R. S., Marshall, H. H., Brattesani, K. A., & Middlestadt, S. E. (1982). Student perceptions of differential teacher treatment in open and traditional classrooms. *Journal of Educational Psychology, 74,* 678-692.

Weinstein, R. S., & Middlestadt, S. E. (1979). Student perceptions of teacher interactions with male high and low achievers. *Journal of Educational Psychology, 71,* 421-431.

Weisz, J. R., & Stipek, D. (1982). Competence, contingency, and the development of perceived control. *Human Development, 25,* 250-281.

Willows, D. M. (1974). Reading between the lines: Selective attention in good and poor readers. *Child Development, 45,* 408-415.

Winne, P. H., & Marx, R. W. (1980). Matching students' cognitive responses to teaching skills. *Journal of Educational Psychology, 72,* 257-264.

Winne, P. H., & Marx, R. W. (1982). Students' and teachers' views of thinking processes for classroom learning. *Elementary School Journal, 82,* 493-518.

Winne, P. H., & Marx, R. W. (1983). *Students' cognitive processes while learning from teaching* (Final Report, NIE-G-0098).Burnaby, British Columbia: Simon Fraser University, Faculty of Education.

Wittrock, M. C. (1963) Response mode in the programming of kinetic molecular theory concepts. *Journal of Educational Psychology, 54,* 89-93.

Wittrock, M. C. (1967). Replacement and nonreplacement strategies in children's problem solving. *Journal of Educational Psychology, 58,* 69-74.

Wittrock, M. C. (1974a). Learning as a generative process. *Educational Psychologist, 11,* 87-95.

Wittrock, M. C. (1974b). A generative model of mathematics learning. *Journal for Research in Mathematics Education, 5,* 181-197.

Wittrock, M. C. (1978). The cognitive movement in instruction. *Educational Psychologist, 13,* 15-30.

Wittrock, M. C. (1981). Reading comprehension. In F. J. Pirozzolo &

M. C. Wittrock (Eds.), *Neuropsychological and cognitive processes of reading.* New York: Academic Press.

Wittrock, M. C. (1983). Writing and the teaching of reading. *Language Arts, 60,* 600–606.

Wittrock, M. C. (in press). Education and recent research on attention and knowledge acquisition. In S. L. Friedman, K. A. Klivington, & R. W. Peterson (Eds.), *Brain, cognition, and education.* New York: Academic Press.

Wittrock, M. C., & Carter, J. (1975). Generative processing of hierarchically organized words. *American Journal of Psychology, 88,* 489–501.

Wittrock, M. C., & Goldberg, S. (1975). Imagery and meaningfulness in free recall; Word attributes and instructional sets. *Journal of General Psychology, 92,* 137–151.

Wittrock, M. C., & Lumsdaine, A. A. (1977). Instructional psychology. In M. R. Rosenzweig & L. W. Porter (Eds.), *Annual Review of Psychology. 28,* 417–459.

Wittrock, M. C., Marks, C. B., & Doctorow, M. J. (1975). Reading as a generative process. *Journal of Educational Psychology, 67,* 484–489.

Yates, F. (1966). *The art of memory.* London: Routledge & Kegan Paul, 1966.

Zeaman, D., & House, B. (1963). The role of attention in retardate discrimination learning. In N. Ellis, *Handbook of mental deficiency.* New York: McGraw-Hill Book Co., p. 159–223.

TEACHERS' THOUGHT PROCESSES

Christopher M. Clark
Penelope L. Peterson

The thinking, planning, and decision making of teachers constitute a large part of the psychological context of teaching. It is within this context that curriculum is interpreted and acted upon; where teachers teach and students learn. Teacher behavior is substantially influenced and even determined by teachers' thought processes. These are the fundamental assumptions behind the literature that has come to be called research on teacher thinking. Practitioners of this branch of educational research seek first to describe fully the mental lives of teachers. Second, they hope to understand and explain how and why the observable activities of teachers' professional lives take on the forms and functions that they do. They ask when and why teaching is difficult, and how human beings manage the complexity of classroom teaching. The ultimate goal of research on teachers' thought processes is to construct a portrayal of the cognitive psychology of teaching for use by educational theorists, researchers, policymakers, curriculum designers, teacher educators, school administrators, and by teachers themselves.

Our aims in this chapter are to offer a framework for organizing research on teachers' thought processes, to summarize and comment upon this diverse body of work, and to make recommendations concerning the future of research on teacher thinking. Earlier reviews of this literature (Clark & Yinger, 1979a; Posner, 1981; Shavelson & Stern, 1981) have been helpful to us in conceptualizing the organization of the field and in identifying the relevant studies. In compiling research reports for this review our main criterion was topical. That is, we searched the

---

The authors thank reviewers Susan Florio-Ruane (Michigan State University), Gaea Leinhardt (University of Pittsburgh), and Robert Yinger (University of Cincinnati).

The two authors contributed equally to the writing of this chapter. The first author was responsible primarily for the sections on teacher planning and teachers' implicit theories. The second author was responsible primarily for the sections on teachers' interactive thoughts and decisions and teachers' attributions. The work of the first author was supported by the Institute for Research on Teaching, Michigan State University, which is funded in part by the National Institute of Education (Contract No. 400-81-0014). The work of the second author was supported by the Wisconsin Center for Education Research, which is funded in part by a grant from the National Institute of Education (Grant No. NIE-G-81-0009). The opinions expressed here are those of the authors.

educational research literature for reports of research on teaching whose titles and abstracts suggested that a primary focus of the research was some aspect of teacher thinking (e.g., planning, decision making, judgment, implicit theories, expectations, attributions). The reports of research included in this review constitute a mixture of published journal articles and less widely available conference papers, technical reports, and doctoral dissertations. It is an indication of the newness of this field that the vast majority of the work has been done since 1976.

Beginnings of Research on Teachers' Thought Processes

In his book *Life in Classrooms* (1968), Philip Jackson reported the results of one of the first studies that attempted to describe and understand the mental constructs and processes that underlie teacher behavior. The descriptive character of his study was a striking departure from contemporary research on teaching and did not fit easily with the then-dominant correlational and experimental research paradigms. In 1968 it was difficult to see how description of life in a few classrooms could contribute much to the quest for teaching effectiveness. But the real power of Jackson's research was not to be found in prescriptions for teaching that might be derived from the work. Rather, Jackson's contribution to research on teaching was conceptual. He portrayed the full complexity of the teacher's task, made conceptual distinctions that fit the teacher's frame of reference (such as that between the preactive and interactive phases of teaching), and called the attention of the educational research community to the importance of describing the thinking and planning of teachers as a means to fuller understanding of classroom processes. In sum, Jackson's (1966) argument was the following:

> A glimpse at this "hidden" side of teaching may increase our understanding of some of the more visible and well-known features of the process.

In Sweden, Dahllof and Lundgren (1970) conducted a series of studies of the structure of the teaching process as an expression of organizational constraints. While this work was primarily concerned with the effects of contextual factors on teaching, it revealed some of the mental categories that teachers use to organize and make sense of their professional experiences. As with Jackson, the Dahllof and Lundgren contribution was primarily conceptual. Of particular significance in the Dahllof and Lundgren research was the phenomenon of the "steering group," a small subset of a class (ranging in achievement level from the 10th to 25th percentiles) that their teachers used as an informal reference group for decisions about pacing a lesson or unit. During whole-class instruction, when the students in the steering group seemed to understand what was being presented, the teacher would move the class on to a new topic. But when the teachers believed that the steering group students were not understanding or performing up to standards, the teachers slowed the pace of instruction for all. The steering group is important as a concept both because of its empirical verifiability and because it shows clearly how teachers' mental constructs can have significant pedagogical consequences.

In June 1974 the National Institute of Education convened a week-long National Conference on Studies in Teaching to create an agenda for future research on teaching. The participants in this planning conference were organized into 10 panels and each panel produced a plan for research in their area of expertise. The deliberations of Panel 6 on "Teaching as Clinical Information Processing" were of importance to the development of research on teacher thinking. Panel 6 was chaired by Lee S. Shulman and included a diverse group of experts on the psychology of human information processing, the anthropology of education, classroom interaction research, and on the practical realities of teaching. Panel 6 produced a report (National Institute of Education, 1975a) that enunciated a rationale for and defined the assumptions and the domain of a proposed program of research on teachers' thought processes. In this report the panelists argued that research on teacher thinking is necessary if we are to understand that which is uniquely human in the process of teaching:

> It is obvious that what teachers do is directed in no small measure by what they think. Moreover, it will be necessary for any innovations in the context, practices, and technology of teaching to be mediated through the minds and motives of teachers. To the extent that observed or intended teacher behavior is "thoughtless," it makes no use of the human teacher's most unique attributes. In so doing, it becomes mechanical and might well be done by a machine. If, however, teaching is done and, in all likelihood, will continue to

be done by human teachers, the question of the relationships between thought and action becomes crucial. (p.1)

Beyond this logical argument for attending to teacher thinking, the Panel 6 report went on to cite research on human information processing, which indicates that a person, when faced with a complex situation, creates a simplified model of that situation and then behaves rationally in relation to that simplified model. Simon claims that "such behavior is not even approximately optimal with respect to the real world. To predict . . . behavior we must understand the way in which this simplified model is constructed, and its construction will certainly be related to (one's) psychological properties as a perceiving, thinking, and learning animal" (Simon, 1957; cited in National Institute of Education, 1975a, p. 2). To understand, predict, and influence what teachers do, the panelists argued, researchers must study the psychological processes by which teachers perceive and define their professional responsibilities and situations.

The Panel 6 report (National Institute of Education, 1975a) is explicit about the view of the teacher that guided the panelists in their deliberations and recommendations for research:

> The Panel was oriented toward the teacher as clinician, not only in the sense of someone diagnosing specific forms of learning dysfunction or pathology and prescribing particular remedies, but more broadly as an individual responsible for (a) aggregating and making sense out of an incredible diversity of information sources about individual students and the class collectively; (b) bringing to bear a growing body of empirical and theoretical work constituting the research literature of education; somehow (c) combining all that information with the teacher's own expectations, attitudes, beliefs, purposes . . . and (d) having to respond, make judgments, render decisions, reflect, and regroup to begin again.

In short, the Panel 6 report presented an image of the teacher as a professional who has more in common with physicians, lawyers, and architects than with technicians who execute skilled performances according to prescriptions or algorithms defined by others. This view of the teacher as professional has had a profound effect on the questions asked, methods of inquiry employed, and the form of the results reported in research on teacher thinking. Moreover, the Panel 6 report influenced new initiatives in research on teaching in a more instrumental way - in 1975 the National Institute of Education issued a request for proposals for an Institute for Research on Teaching that would focus on research on teaching as clinical information processing. An Institute for Research on Teaching was established at Michigan State University in 1976, and this organization initiated the first large program of research on the thought processes of teachers.

A Model of Teacher Thought and Action

A major goal of research on teacher thought processes is to increase our understanding of how and why the process of teaching looks and works as it does. To assist the reader in visualizing how the several parts of the research literature on teacher thought processes relate to one another and how research on teacher thought processes complements the larger body of research on teaching effectiveness, we have developed the model of teacher thought and action presented in Figure 1. We make no claims for the empirical validity of this model, but rather offer it as a heuristic device that may be useful in making sense of the literature and as an "advance organizer" for the topics and information that we will present in this chapter.

The model depicts two domains that are importantly involved in the process of teaching. Each domain is represented by a circle. These domains are (a) teachers' thought processes, and (b) teachers' actions and their observable effects. These two domains differ in at least two important ways. First, the domains differ in the extent to which the processes involved are observable. Teachers' thought processes occur "inside teachers' heads" and thus are unobservable. In contrast, teacher behavior, student behavior, and student achievement scores constitute observable phenomena. Thus, the phenomena involved in the teacher action domain are more easily measured and more easily subjected to empirical research methods than are the phenomena involved in the teacher thought domain. As we shall see in the next section on methods of inquiry, the domain of teachers' thought processes presents challenging methodological problems for the empirical researcher. Second, the two domains represent two paradigmatic approaches to research on

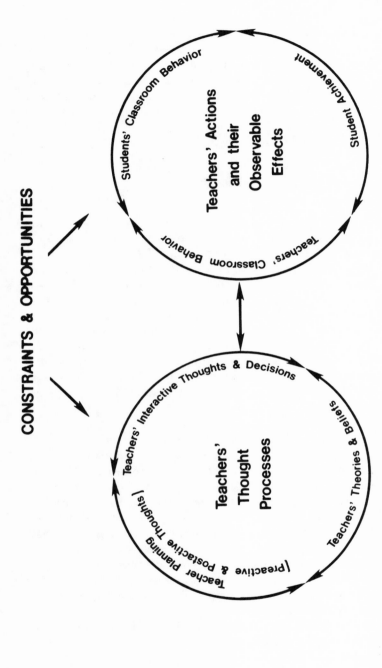

Fig. 1. A model of teacher thought and action.

CONSTRAINTS & OPPORTUNITIES

Teachers' Actions and their Observable Effects

Students' Classroom Behavior

Student Achievement

Teachers' Classroom Behavior

Teachers' Thought Processes

Teachers' Interactive Thoughts & Decisions

Teachers' Theories & Beliefs

Teacher Planning (Preactive & Postactive Thoughts)

teaching. Prior to 1975, the dominant research paradigm was the process-product approach to the study of teaching effectiveness. Process-product researchers have been concerned primarily with the relationship between teachers' classroom behavior, students' classroom behavior, and student achievement. In contrast, the domain of research on teachers' thought processes constitutes a paradigmatic approach to research on teaching which has only recently emerged. We will now briefly describe each domain.

Teachers' Actions and Their Observable Effects

The action domain is where classroom teaching actually takes place. Teachers behave in certain ways in the classroom and their behavior has observable effects on students. Process-product researchers have typically assumed that causality is unidirectional, with teachers' classroom behavior affecting students' classroom behavior, which ultimately affects students' achievement (see, for example, Doyle, 1977b; Dunkin & Biddle, 1974). In the model shown in Figure 1, we assume that the relationships between teacher behavior, student behavior, and student achievement are reciprocal. Moreover, rather than representing the direction of causation as linear, we think that it is more accurate to represent the direction of causation as cyclical or circular. Our circular model of teachers' actions and their observable effects thus allows for the possibility that teacher behavior affects student behavior, which in turn affects teacher behavior and ultimately student achievement. Alternatively, students' achievement may cause teachers to behave differently toward the student, which then affects student behavior and subsequent student achievement.

The relationships between the three variables in the domain of teacher actions have been investigated systematically by researchers on teaching effectiveness. This research is summarized and described by Brophy and Good (this volume). Unfortunately, however, most of this research has assumed that the relationship between teachers' actions and their observable affects is a linear one and is unidirectional, and most research has not explored the possibility of reciprocal effects as we suggest in our model.

Teachers' Thought Processes

Three major categories of teachers' thought processes are encompassed within this domain: (a) teacher planning (preactive and postactive thoughts); (b) teachers' interactive thoughts and decisions; and (c) teachers' theories and beliefs. These categories reflect the researchers' conceptualization of the domain of teachers' thought processes more than an empirically derived categorization of the domain. The first two categories represent a temporal distinction between whether the thought processes occur during classroom interaction (i.e., teachers' interactive thoughts and decisions) or before or after classroom interaction (i.e., preactive and postactive thoughts). These categories follow from Jackson's (1968) distinction between the preactive, interactive, and postactive phases of teaching. These distinctions were first used by Crist, Marx, and Peterson (1974) as a way of categorizing teachers' thought processes because these researchers hypothesized that the kind of thinking that teachers do during classroom interaction would be qualitatively different from the kinds of thinking that teachers do before and after classroom interaction.

As we will see in our review of research on teachers' thought processes, the distinction between teachers' interactive thoughts and decisions and their preactive thoughts and decisions has been retained by researchers and appears to be an important one. The kind of thinking that teachers do during interactive teaching does appear to be qualitatively different from the kind of thinking they do when they are not interacting with students. In contrast, the distinction between teachers' preactive and postactive thoughts does not seem to have been retained by researchers. These two categories have been subsumed under the category of "teacher planning." Teacher planning includes the thought processes that teachers engage in prior to classroom interaction but also includes the thought processes or reflections that they engage in after classroom interaction that then guide their thinking and projections for future classroom interaction. For example, teacher planning includes the reflections that the teacher has at 3:30 p.m. at the end of a given day that then cause the teacher to plan a certain activity for the class for 8:30 a.m. the next morning. Thus, because the teaching process is a cyclical one the distinction between preactive and postactive thoughts has become blurred.

The third category, teachers' theories and beliefs, represents the rich store of knowledge that teachers have that affects their planning and their interactive thoughts and decisions. The arrows in the model indicate these effects. Of course, teachers may also develop theories and beliefs as a result of their thinking during classroom interaction and of their planning prior to and following classroom interaction. Thus, as the arrows in the model indicate, teachers' interactive thoughts and decisions and teacher planning, respectively, may also affect teachers' thoughts and beliefs.

We have included these three categories of teachers' thought processes — teacher planning, teachers' interactive thoughts and decisions, and teachers' theories and beliefs — because to date the research on teachers' thought processes has been directed toward these three major topics. In our model and in our subsequent review of the research on teachers' thought processes, we have chosen not to separate out a fourth category, teacher judgment, which has been treated as a distinct category by earlier reviewers of this research. (See, for example, Clark & Yinger, 1979a; Shavelson & Stern, 1981). We decided not to discuss research on teacher judgment as a separate category because teacher judgment is but one cognitive process that teachers use in their planning and interactive decision making. Thus, we have subsumed the research on teacher judgment under the appropriate category of teacher planning, teachers' interactive thoughts and decisions, or teachers' theories and beliefs.

In sum, the three categories in the domain of teachers' thought processes reflect the state of the field in research on teachers' thought processes and thus reflect the researchers' conceptualizations of the field. For this reason, we have chosen to use these three categories as the organizing topics for our review of the research literature.

Constraints and Opportunities

A complete understanding of the process of teaching is not possible without an understanding of the constraints and opportunities that impinge upon the teaching process. Teachers' actions are often constrained by the physical setting or by external influences such as the school, the principal, the community, or the curriculum. Conversely, teachers may be able to behave in a certain way simply because they are given a rare opportunity to do so. Teacher's thought processes may be similarly constrained. For example, teachers may have less flexibility in their planning or perceive that they have less flexibility in their planning because certain curriculum decisions have been made already by the school district or by the principal. Alternatively, other principals may give teachers more flexibility and opportunity to engage in planning and decision making. Indeed, the extent to which responsibility and participation in the decision-making process are given to teachers (here defined as constraints and opportunities) has been shown to be an important variable that defines effective schools. (See, for example, Good and Brophy, this volume). Therefore, we deem this variable an important one that needs to be included in any model of the process of teaching. Moreover, as we shall see in our review of the research on teachers' thought processes, research findings suggest that teachers' thought processes are affected profoundly by the task demands and by the teachers' perceptions of the task. We view task demands as encompassed within constraints and opportunities.

The Relationship Between the Domains of Teacher Thought and Action

As the double-headed arrow between the domains of teacher thought and action in our model indicates, there is a reciprocal relationship between these two domains. Teachers' actions are in a large part caused by teachers' thought processes, which then in turn affect teachers' actions. However, we contend that the process of teaching will be fully understood only when these two domains are brought together and examined in relation to one another. We hope that the model presented in Figure 1 will serve as a useful step toward achieving such a synoptic view of the process of teaching and will also aid the reader in understanding the topics and issues that we address in the remainder of this chapter.

In the remainder of this chapter, we will review and discuss the research that has been done on teacher planning, teachers' interactive thoughts and decisions, and teachers' theories and beliefs. Before beginning our review, however, we provide a brief overview of the several methods of inquiry that have been used in research on teachers' thought processes.

Methods of Inquiry

The systematic study of the thought processes of teachers demands that researchers deal with serious technical, methodological, and epistemological challenges. This research depends heavily on various forms of self-report by teachers, and the central methodological problem deals with how to elicit and interpret valid and reliable self-reports about cognitive processes. The use of verbal reports as data has been criticized by Nisbett and Wilson (1977), and their arguments have been challenged by Ericcson and Simon (1980). Ericcson and Simon indicated that verbal reports will be most reliable and valid as data when a person is reporting on the contents of short-term memory, that is, that which he or she is currently attending to. Less reliable and valid data will result from probes that are vague and general or that require respondents to use inferential processes to complete or elaborate partially remembered information.

In the studies reviewed in this chapter, the researchers usually employed various combinations of five methods of inquiry: thinking aloud, stimulated recall, policy capturing, journal keeping and the repertory grid technique. Often these methods were supplemented by interviews, field observations, and narrative descriptions of the task, the context, and the visible behavior of the participants in a study. We will briefly describe each of these methods. (Shavelson, Webb & Burstein, this volume, discuss these methods further.)

Thinking Aloud

The thinking aloud method consists of having a teacher verbalize all of his or her thoughts while engaged in a task such as planning a lesson (e.g., Peterson, Marx, & Clark, 1978) or making judgments about curriculum materials (e.g., Yinger & Clark, 1982). The teacher's verbalizations are recorded, usually on audiotape but occasionally on videotape (e.g., Smith & Sendelbach, 1979), and later transcribed to create typewritten protocols. The protocols are then subjected to various kinds of coding systems (almost always created by the investigator) to produce descriptions of the content of teacher thinking and of the sequences of cognitive processes that teachers follow while planning, making decisions, and teaching.

Stimulated Recall

The stimulated recall method was used originally by Bloom (1954) and consists of replaying a videotape or audiotape of a teaching episode to enable the viewer (usually the teacher of the episode) to recollect and report on his or her thoughts and decisions during the teaching episode. Variations in the use of stimulated recall include replaying only researcher-selected portions of the recording versus replaying the complete tape; researchers asking prespecified questions each time the tape is stopped versus soliciting open-ended commentary from the teacher; and researcher control of when to stop the tape versus teacher control or shared control. The teacher's reports and comments about thoughts and decisions while teaching are audiotaped, transcribed, and subjected to content analysis. Conners (1978a) and Tuckwell (1980a, 1980b) provide a summary, analysis, and recommendations regarding techniques for conducting stimulated recall sessions and analyses of the resulting protocols. Calderhead (1981) offers a more theoretical and philosophical analysis of the limits and possibilities of stimulated recall in the study of teaching.

Policy Capturing

Policy capturing is a method borrowed from laboratory psychology (e.g., Hammond, 1971; Rappoport & Summers, 1973) for use in studying teacher judgment processes. In a typical policy capturing study, a teacher is presented with a series of printed descriptions of students or of hypothetical teaching situations or of curricular materials. These descriptions have been edited by the researchers so that all possible combinations of as many as five features or "cues" appear in the full set of objects to be judged. The teacher is asked to make one or more judgements or decisions about each printed description, usually recorded on a Likert scale. The goal of this approach is to produce mathematical models (usually linear regression equations) that describe the relative weightings that teachers attach to the features of the objects being judged as they make judgments about them. The resulting equations represent the "policy" of the teacher in relation to the domain in which the judgments were made (e.g., assignment of students to reading groups, selection of curricular materials). Of the several methods used to study teacher thinking, policy capturing depends least on teacher self-reports. However, the method is limited to relatively simple judgment situations that involve a small number of cues or features (typically five or fewer) that can be identified a priori by the researchers. (See Yinger and Clark, 1982 for a comparison of the strengths and limitations of policy capturing and think aloud methods in research on teaching.)

Journal Keeping

The primary application of journal keeping in research on teacher thinking has been in the study of planning. Teachers are typically asked to keep a written record of their plans for instruction as they develop, and to comment in writing on (a) the context in which their plans are made, (b) their reasons for selecting one course of action over another, and (c) their reflections on and evaluation of their plans after they are brought into action in the classroom. Journal keeping is usually supplemented by frequent interviews, both to encourage and support the teacher in the often demanding and unfamiliar process of journal keeping and to clarify and elaborate unclear or incomplete journal entries. In some cases, the researcher enters into a written dialogue with the teacher in the pages of the journal. Journal entries are subjected to content analyses and the data are used to generate descriptions and models of the planning process and the factors that influence it. (For a discussion of the use of dialogue journals see Staton, 1982.) Yinger and Clark (1981, 1985) discuss theoretical and practical issues in the use of journal writing in research on teaching.

The Repertory Grid Technique

The repertory grid technique has been used in the study of teachers' implicit theories. This technique was developed by Kelly (1955) as a method for discovering the personal constructs that influence individual behavior. An individual is presented with a series of cards on which are written single words or statements about the domain of interest to the investigator. The subject is asked to indicate which cards are alike or different and to explain why. The resulting groupings and their associated rationales are labeled as "constructs" by the investigator. The constructs and their component elements are then arrayed in a grid format to show (either by inspection or through factor analysis) the relationships among constructs. Variations in the repertory grid technique include having the respondent generate the elements to be sorted (e.g., Munby, 1983) and involving the respondent in analysis of the relationships among components through clinical interviews (e.g., Olson, 1981).

Teacher Planning

Researchers have conceptualized teacher planning in two ways. First, they have thought of planning as a set of basic psychological processes in which a person visualizes the future, inventories means and ends, and constructs a framework to guide his or her future action. This conception of planning draws heavily on the theories and methods of cognitive psychology. Second, researchers have defined planning as "the things that teachers do when they say that they are planning." This definition suggests a phenomonological or descriptive approach to research on teacher planning, in which the teacher takes on an important role as informant or even as research collaborator.

Both of these views of teacher planning are represented in the research literature either explicitly or implicitly. These two different starting points for the study of teacher planning probably account for the variety of methods of inquiry in use and for the challenge that reviewers of this literature face in pulling together a coherent summary of what has been learned. Planning is challenging to study because it is both a psychological process and a practical activity.

We have organized our review of the research on teacher planning to address three major questions: (a) What are the types and functions of teacher planning? (b) What models have been used to describe the process of planning? and (c) What is the relationship between teacher planning and the teacher's subsequent actions in the classroom?

Types and Functions of Teacher Planning

What are the different kinds of planning that teachers do, and what purposes do they serve? The answer to both parts of this question seems to be "many." That is, many different kinds of planning are in use, and they serve many functions.

TYPES OF PLANNING

Table 1 summarizes the findings of eight studies in which researchers investigated the types and functions of teacher planning. Yinger (1977) and Clark and Yinger (1979b) determined that during the course of a school year, experienced teachers engaged in as many as eight different types of planning. The names of six of these eight types designate a span of time for which the planning took place: weekly, daily, long range, short range, yearly, and term planning. The remaining two types (unit and lesson planning) describe a unit of content for which the teachers planned. Judging from these empirically derived typologies of teacher planning, we would conclude that substantial teacher energy is devoted to structuring, organizing for, and managing limited classroom instructional time.

Yinger's (1977) finding that routines are a principal product of teacher planning (also supported by the work of Bromme, 1982 and Creemers & Westerhof, 1982) suggests that teachers respond to the press for simplification and efficient time management by planning. Yinger defined routines as sets of established procedures for both teacher and students that function to control and coordinate specific sequences of behavior. He identified four types of routines as products of teacher planning: (a) activity routines, (b) instructional routines, (c) management routines, and (d) executive planning routines. Routines "played such a major role in the teacher's planning behavior that [such] planning could be characterized as decision making about the selection, organization, and sequencing of routines" (1979, p. 165).

The relative importance of different types of planning was also explored by Clark and Yinger (1979b). Unit planning was cited most often by the teachers as most important, followed by weekly and daily planning. Only 7% of the teachers in this study listed lesson planning among the three most important types.

Table 1. Summary of Findings of Eight Studies of the Types and Functions of Teacher Planning

Study	Method of Inquiry	Teachers	Subject Matter	Principal Findings
Clark & Elmore (1979)	Observation, interview, and journal keeping	5 teachers of grades K–5	All	Planning early in school year focuses on establishing the physical environment and social system of the classroom.
Clark & Elmore (1981)	Think aloud during yearly planning	1 teacher of grade 2	Mathematics, science, writing	Functions of yearly planning: (a) to adapt curriculum to fit teacher's knowledge and priorities, and unique classroom situation; (b) for teacher to learn the structure and content of new curricula; (c) to develop a practical schedule for instruction.
Clark & Yinger (1979b)	Written description of plans by teachers	78 elementary teachers	All	1. Eight types of planning: weekly, daily, unit, long range, lesson, short range, yearly, term. 2. Three most important types: unit, weekly, daily. 3. Planning functions to (a) meet immediate psychological needs of the planner, (b) prepare the teacher cognitively and instrumentally for instruction, and (c) guide the interactive processes of instruction.
McCutcheon (1980)	Ethnography	12 teachers of Grades 1–6	All	1. Much teacher planning is never put on paper. 2. Functions of written lesson plans: (a) to meet administrators' demands,

Study	Method	Sample	Subject area	Findings
				and (b) to be used by substitute teachers.
				3. Long-range planning viewed as counterproductive because of unpredictable changes in schedule and interruptions.
Morine-Dershimer (1977)	Observation, analysis of written plans and interview	20 teachers of Grade 2; 20 teachers of Grade 5	Reading, mathematics	1. Most lesson planning done mentally rather than on paper. 2. Outline or list of topics most typical form of plan.
Morine-Dershimer (1979)	Interview, observation, and stimulated recall	10 elementary teachers		1. Mental "image" of a lesson plan used to guide teacher behavior during routine instruction. 2. Lesson plan largely abandoned when activity flow is threatened with disruption.
Smith & Sendelbach (1979)	Observation, think aloud, and stimulated recall	4 teachers of Grade 6	Science	1. Teachers depend heavily on published teacher's guides. 2. Planning produces a mental image of the unit to be taught. 3. While teaching, the teacher tries to recall and enact this mental image of the plan (with very little of the plan on paper).
Yinger (1977)	Ethnography, observation, and interview	1 teacher of combined Grades 1 & 2	All	1. Five types of planning: yearly, term, unit, weekly, and daily. 2. The "activity" was the basic unit and starting point for planning. 3. Routines are used to simplify complexity for both teacher and students.

Researchers have also investigated the dynamic relationships among different types of planning. Morine-Dershimer (1977, 1979) found that teachers' written plans seldom reflect the teachers' entire plan. Rather, the few details recorded on a written plan were nested within more comprehensive planning structures, called "lesson images" by Morine-Dershimer. These lesson images, in turn, were nested within a still larger construct called the "activity flow" by Joyce (1978–1979). For elementary teachers, the activity flow encompasses the yearlong progress of a class through each particular subject matter and also is concerned with the balance of activities across subject matters in a school day or week.

Further support for the idea that teacher planning is a nested process comes from a study by Clark and Elmore (1979). Clark and Elmore interviewed and observed five elementary teachers during the first five weeks of the school year and found that teachers' planning was concerned primarily with setting up the physical environment of the classroom, assessing student abilities, and establishing the social system of the classroom. By the end of the fourth week of school, teachers had established a system of schedules, routines, and groupings for instruction. These structural and social features of the classroom then persisted throughout the school year and served as the framework within which teachers planned particular activities and units. Other studies of the first weeks of school also support the conclusion that, to a significant degree, the "problem space" (Newell & Simon, 1972) within which teacher and students operate is defined early, changes little during the course of the school year, and exerts a powerful, if subtle, influence on thought and behavior (e.g., Anderson & Evertson, 1978; Buckley & Cooper, 1978; Shultz & Florio, 1979; Tikunoff & Ward, 1978).

FUNCTIONS OF PLANNING

Findings from research on teacher planning suggest that teachers have as many reasons to plan as they have types of planning. Clark and Yinger (1979b) found that teachers' written responses to a question about why they plan fell into three clusters: (a) planning to meet immediate personal needs (e.g., to reduce uncertainty and anxiety, to find a sense of direction, confidence, and security); (b) planning as a means to the end of instruction (e.g., to learn the material, to collect and organize materials, to organize time and activity flow); and (c) planning to serve a direct function during instruction (e.g., to organize students, to get an activity started, to aid memory, to provide a framework for instruction and evaluation).

In an ethnographic study of the planning of 12 elementary teachers, McCutcheon (1980) confirmed that some teachers plan to meet the administrative requirement that they turn in their plans to the school principal on a regular basis. These teachers also indicated that special plans were necessary for use by substitute teachers in the event of absence of the regular teacher. These plans for substitute teachers were special both because they included a great deal of background information about how "the system" in a particular classroom and school operated and because the regular teachers tended to reserve the teaching of what they judged to be important material for themselves, and they planned filler or drill and practice activities for the substitute teachers.

PLANNING AND THE CONTENT
OF INSTRUCTION

The most obvious function of teacher planning in American schools is to transform and modify curriculum to fit the unique circumstances of each teaching situation. In one of the only studies of yearly planning, Clark and Elmore (1981) asked a second grade teacher to think aloud while doing her yearly planning for mathematics, science, and writing. The teacher reported that the primary resources that she used in her yearly planning were curriculum materials (especially the teacher's guides), memory of classroom interaction during the previous year, and the calendar for the coming school year. Her process of yearly planning, typically done during the summer months, consisted of reviewing the curriculum materials that she would be using during the coming year, rearranging the sequence of topics within curricula, and adding and deleting content to be taught. A broad outline of the content to be taught and, to a lesser extent, of how it would be taught, emerged from a process of mental review of the events of the past year, combined with adjustment of the planned sequence and pace of teaching to accommodate new curriculum materials and new ideas consistent with her implicit theory of instruction. Through her review of the past year, reflection on her satisfaction with how things went, and modifications of the content, sequence, and planned pace of instruction, the teacher's yearly planning process served to integrate her own experiences with the published materials, establishing a sense of ownership and control of content to be taught (Ben-Peretz, 1975). Yearly planning sessions satisfied this teacher that she had available the resources to provide conditions for learning that would be at least equal to those that she had provided during the previous year. For this teacher, yearly planning decreased the unpredictability and uncertainty that attend every teaching situation.

The Clark and Elmore (1981) study of yearly planning supports the idea that published curriculum materials have a powerful influence on the content and process of teaching. In a study of teacher planning for sixth grade science instruction, Smith and Sendelbach (1979) pursued this idea at the level of unit planning. Working with the Science Curriculum Improvement Study (SCIS) science curriculum, Smith and Sendelbach compared explicit directions for a unit of instruction provided in the teacher's manual with four teachers' transformations of those directions into plans, and finally with the actual classroom behavior of one of the four teachers while teaching the unit. Observation of the four teachers during planning sessions combined with analysis of think aloud and stimulated recall interview data revealed that the principal product of a unit-planning session was a mental picture of the unit to be taught, the sequence of activitities within it, and the students' probable responses. These mental plans were supplemented and cued by sketchy notes and lists of important points that the teachers wanted to be sure to remember. Smith and Sendelbach characterized the process of activating a unit plan as one of reconstructing the plan from memory, rather than of carefully following the directions provided in the teacher's guide.

Smith and Sendelbach argued that the lack of a strong connection between the published curriculum and instruction created the potential for distortions or significant omissions in the content of science instruction. From their classroom observations of one experienced teacher implementing her unit plan, they concluded that the quality of instruction was degraded somewhat by both planned and unintended deviations from the SCIS curriculum. They attributed these deviations to the teacher's limited subject matter knowledge, difficulty in finding information in the teacher's guide, and to the presence of inherently complex and confusing concepts.

Three points are of special interest concerning the types and functions of teacher planning. First, researchers on teacher planning have tended to focus on a single type of planning and to study teachers at only the elementary level. To fully understand the task demands of teaching and the ways in which teachers respond to these demands, researchers need to describe the full range of kinds of planning that teachers do during the school year and the interrelationships between these kinds of planning. Second, the modest-to-insignificant role of lesson planning reported by experienced teachers is interesting. Lesson planning is the one type of planning that is addressed directly in all teacher preparation programs. Yet lesson planning is rarely claimed as an important part of the repertoire of experienced teachers. Perhaps differences between expert and novice teachers dictate that teacher education focus heavily on lesson planning. But this anomaly may also indicate that some of our teacher preparation practices bow more to the task demands of the university calendar, methods courses, and supervision models than to those of the public school environment. Finally, the functions of teacher planning that are not directly and exclusively concerned with a particular instructional episode seem to have been slighted in the research literature. Researchers and teacher educators should think more broadly about what teachers are accomplishing in their planning time, and avoid narrow comparisons of what was planned with what was taught as the major criterion for evaluation of planning quality.

Models that Describe Teacher Planning

The second major goal of researchers on teacher planning is to create models that describe the planning process. The logic of an industrial production system underlies the most widely prescribed model for teacher planning, first proposed by Ralph Tyler (1950). This linear model consists of a sequence of four steps: (a) specify objectives; (b) select learning activities; (c) organize learning activities; and (d) specify evaluation procedures. This linear model has been recommended for use at all levels of educational planning, and thousands of educators have been trained in its use. It was not until 1970 that researchers began to examine directly the planning processes in use by teachers and to compare what was being practiced with what was prescribed. Table 2 summarizes the studies conducted by these researchers.

Taylor's (1970) study of teacher planning in British secondary schools was directed toward examining how teachers planned syllabi for courses. Using group discussions with teachers, analyses of course syllabi, and a questionnaire administered to 261 teachers of English, science, and geography, Taylor came to the following general conclusions: The most common theme in the teachers' course planning was the prominence of the pupil, especially pupil needs, abilities, and interests. Following the pupil as a focus of planning, in order of importance, were the subject matter, goals, and teaching methods. In planning for courses of study, teachers attributed little importance to evaluation and to the relationship between their own courses and the curriculum as a whole.

Taylor described the course-planning process as one in which the teacher begins with the context of teaching; next considers learning situations likely to interest and involve pupils; and only after this, considers the purposes that teaching would serve. Taylor indicated that teachers gave minor importance to the criteria and procedures for evaluating the effectiveness of their course of teaching. Taylor concluded that in curriculum planning teachers should begin with the content to be taught and accompanying important contextual considerations (e.g., time, sequencing, resources). Teachers should then consider pupil interests and attitudes, aims and purposes of the course, learning situations to be created, the philosophy of the course, the criteria for judging the course, the degree of pupil interest fostered by the course, and finally, evaluation of the course.

Zahorik (1975) continued this line of inquiry in a study in which he asked 194 teachers to list in writing the decisions that they made prior to teaching, and to indicate the order in which they made them. He classified these decisions into the following categories: objectives, content, pupil activities, materials, diagnosis, evaluation, instruction, and organization. He found that the kind of decision mentioned by the greatest number of teachers concerned pupil activities (81%). The decision most frequently made first was content (51%), followed by learning objectives (28%). Zahorik concluded that teachers' planning decisions do not always follow linearly from a specification of objectives and that, in fact, objectives are not a particularly important planning decision in terms of quantity of use.

More recently, researchers have turned their attention to describing teacher planning by observing and audiotaping teachers' thinking aloud during planning sessions. Peterson, Marx, and Clark (1978) examined planning in a laboratory situation as 12 teachers prepared to teach a new instructional unit to small groups of junior high school students with whom they had had no previous contact. During their planning periods, teachers were instructed to think aloud, and their verbal statements were later coded into planning categories including objectives, materials, subject matter, and instructional process. The primary findings of this study were: (a) Teachers spent the largest proportion of their planning time dealing with the content to be taught; (b) after subject matter, teachers concentrated their planning efforts on instructional processes (strategies and activities); and (c) teachers spent the smallest proportion of their planning time on objectives. All three of these findings were consistent with those by Zahorik (1975) and Goodlad and Klein (1970). The third finding was also similar to results reported by Joyce and Harootunian (1964) and by Popham and Baker (1970).

In interpreting the Peterson, Marx, and Clark (1978) study, we need to consider the task demands on the teachers. The researchers provided the teachers with unfamiliar materials from which to teach, and they limited preparation time to 90 minutes immediately preceding teaching on each day of the study. Because the teachers did not know their students in advance, the teachers may have placed more emphasis on content and instructional processes in their planning than would normally be the case. Finally, the researchers provided the teachers with a list of six general teaching goals, expressed in terms of content coverage, process goals, and cognitive and attitudinal outcomes for students. Under these circumstances, it is not surprising that the teachers devoted little planning time to composing more specific objectives and used the largest part of their planning time to study the content and decide how to teach it.

Morine-Dershimer and Vallance (1976) found results consistent with those of Peterson, Marx, and Clark. Morine-Dershimer and Vallance collected written plans for two experimenter-prescribed lessons (one in mathematics and one in reading) taught by 20 teachers of second and fifth grades in their own classrooms to a small group of their students. The researchers described teachers' plans in terms of (a) specificity of written plans, (b) general format of plans, (c) statement of

Table 2. Ten Studies of the Planning Process: Summary of Findings

Study	Method of Inquiry	Teachers	Subject Matter	Principal Findings
Clark & Yinger (1979b)	Journal keeping, interviews, and observations	5 elementary teachers	Writing	Two styles of planning consistent with the general features of Yinger's model: 1. Comprehensive planning 2. Incremental planning
Favor-Lydecker (1981)	Think aloud	7 upper elementary teachers and four undergraduates	Social studies	Five different styles of planning
McLeod (1981)	Stimulated recall	17 kindergarten teachers	Various	1. Intended learning outcomes considered during planning, while teaching, and after teaching 2. Types of intended learning outcomes: Cognitive—57.7% Social/affective—35% Psychomotor/perceptual—7.2%
Morine-Dershimer & Vallance (1976)	Analysis of written plans for an experimenter-prescribed lesson	20 teachers of second and fifth grades	Reading and mathematics	1. Outline form for most plans; fairly specific 2. Little attention to behavioral goals, diagnosis of student needs, evaluation, or alternative courses of action
Neale, Pace & Case (1983)	Questionnaire and interview	19 elementary teachers and 9 student teachers	Elementary planning	1. Attitudes toward systematic planning model favorable by teachers and student teachers 2. Belief of experienced teachers that the systematic model is useful primarily for novices and, occasionally, when planning a new

Study	Method	Sample	Subject	Findings
				3. Use by student teachers of systematic planning model only when required to
Peterson, Marx, & Clark (1978)	Think aloud; teaching in laboratory setting	12 junior high school teachers	Social studies	1. Largest proportion of planning time on content 2. Smaller proportion on instructional strategies and activities 3. Smallest on objectives
Sardo (1982)	Observation and interview	4 junior high school teachers	English, mathematics, social studies, Spanish/French	1. Least experienced teacher planned according to Tyler linear model 2. "Content" decisions most frequently made first in planning (51%), followed by learning objectives (28%)
Taylor (1970)	Group discussions, analysis of course syllabi, and exam questions	261 British secondary teachers	English, science, geography	1. Major focus of planning, in order of importance: (a) pupil needs, abilities, and interests; (b) subject matter; (c) goals; (d) teaching methods 2. Evaluation of little importance in course planning 3. Little concern for relationship of planned course to the curriculum as a whole
Yinger (1977)	Ethnography, observation, and interview	1 teacher of combined Grades 1 & 2	All	Three-stage cyclical planning model: 1. Problem finding 2. Problem formulation and solution 3. Implementation, evaluation, and routinization
Zahorik (1975)	Questionnaire	194 elementary teachers	Elementary planning	1. "Pupil activities" the most frequently reported focus of planning (81%) 2. "Content" decisions most frequently made first in planning (51%), followed by learning objectives (28%)

goals, (d) source of goal statements, (e) attention to pupil background and preparation, (f) identification of evaluation procedures, and (g) indication of possible alternative procedures. Teachers tended to be fairly specific and use an outline form in their plans. Their written plans reflected little attention to behavioral goals, diagnosis of student needs, evaluation procedures, and alternative courses of action. However, the teachers reported that writing plans for researcher-prescribed lessons was not typical of their planning, and observations of their classroom teaching behavior revealed that much of what the teachers had planned was not reflected in their written outlines (Morine-Dershimer, 1979).

In his five-month field study of one teacher, Yinger (1977) drew on his observations, interview data, and think aloud protocols to create a theoretical model of the process of teacher planning. He viewed teacher planning as taking place in three stages. The first stage is a discovery cycle in which the teacher's goal conceptions, knowledge and experience, notion of the planning dilemma, and the materials available for planning interact to produce an initial problem conception worthy of further exploration. The second stage is problem formulation and solution. Yinger proposed that the mechanism for carrying out this process is the "design cycle." He characterized problem solving as a design process involving progressive elaboration of plans over time. Moreover, he proposed that elaboration, investigation, and adaptation are the phases through which teachers formulate their plans. The third stage of the planning model involves implementation, evaluation, and eventual routinization of the plan. Yinger emphasized that evaluation and routinization contribute to the teacher's repertoire of knowledge and experience which in turn play a major role in the teacher's future planning deliberations.

A significant contribution of Yinger's way of conceptualizing the planning process is that he proposes a cyclical rather than a linear model. He postulates a recursive design cycle similar to the processes hypothesized to go on in the work of architects, physicians, artists, designers, and other professionals. In addition, he acknowledges that schooling is not a series of unrelated planning-teaching episodes, but that each planning event can be influenced by prior planning and teaching experiences and that, potentially, each teaching event feeds into future planning and teaching processes. He represents the cycle as a continuous, yearlong process, in which the boundaries between planning, teaching, and reflection are not sharp and distinct.

In a further investigation of the Yinger model, Clark and Yinger (1979b) asked five elementary teachers to design and plan a 2-week unit on writing that the teachers had never taught before. The teachers kept journals documenting their plans and their thinking about planning during a 3-week period, and they were interviewed twice each week. The journal keeping and interviews continued and were supplemented by observations during the 2-week period when the teachers were implementing their plans.

Clark and Yinger described the teachers' unit planning as a cyclical process, typically beginning with a general idea and moving through phases of successive elaboration. This tendency of teachers to mentally visualize, elaborate, and modify their plans was further supported by data from a later study of teacher judgment while planning (Yinger & Clark, 1982, 1983). In that study, six teachers who thought aloud while making judgments about published language arts activity descriptions were seen to change and adapt the activity descriptions to fit their own teaching situations and experiences before passing judgment about the quality and usefulness of the activities.

Visualization of the teaching activity being enacted in the specific context of their own classrooms seemed to be an essential feature of the planning process for these experienced elementary school teachers. One could hypothesize that the availability of detailed knowledge structures about a particular teaching setting provides the experienced teacher with the tools for mentally trying out learning activities and distinguishes the expert planner from the novice.

In the Clark and Yinger (1979b) study of unit planning two of the teachers' unit plans consisted of a short problem finding stage, brief unit planning, and considerable reliance on trying out activities in the classroom. Clark and Yinger referred to this approach as "incremental planning" and described teachers who employed a series of short planning steps, relying heavily on day-to-day information from the classroom. They characterized the remaining three unit plans as products of "comprehensive planning," in which the teachers developed a thoroughly specified framework for future action. When compared with incremental planning, comprehensive planning involved more attention to the unit as a whole, and more time and energy invested in specifying plans as completely as possible before beginning to teach. Both approaches to unit planning seemed to work well for the teachers who used them. Incremental planning saved time and energy while staying in touch with changing student states. Comprehensive planning providing a complete and dependable guide for teacher–student interaction for the whole course of a unit, reducing uncertainty and increasing the probability of achieving prespecified learning objectives.

This notion of "planning styles" of teachers was examined further by Sardo (1982). She found a relationship between individual differences in planning style and amount of teaching experience. Sardo studied the planning of four junior high school teachers who varied in teaching experience from 2 years to 30 years. The planning of the least experienced teacher consisted primarily of daily and lesson planning and followed the Tyler linear model most closely, while the more experienced teachers tended to be less systematic planners, to spend less time planning, and to concern themselves with planning the flow of activities for an entire week rather than with the fine details of each lesson.

Similarly, Favor-Lydecker (1981) studied the social studies unit planning styles of 17 teachers of upper elementary grades (4–6) and of four advanced undergraduate elementary education majors. Each of the 21 teachers thought aloud during a 2-hour planning session for a unit on ethnic heritage. Favor-Lydecker described five different planning styles that characterized the 21 unit plans: (a) teacher–student cooperative planning, (b) brainstorming, (c) list and sequence planning, (d) culminating event in sequence planning, and (e) culminating event as goal statement planning.

One recent study tested the possibility that the reported rarity of use of the Tyler model of planning might be due to inadequate training of teachers in its use or to unsupportive contextual factors. In an interview study, Neale, Pace, and Case (1983) contrasted student teachers ($n = 9$) and experienced elementary and special education teachers ($n = 19$) in their attitudes toward and use of the Tyler systematic planning model. They found that both undergraduates and experienced teachers expressed moderately favorable attitudes toward the systematic planning model, but that experienced teachers believed that it was useful mainly for student teachers and not for themselves. Five of the 19 experienced teachers reported using the systematic planning model only when developing a new unit, and the remaining 14 teachers reported that they did not use the model at all because they believed that it took too much time, was unnecessary, or was implicitly rather than explicitly included in their informal planning. The student teachers reported that they followed the systematic planning model closely when they were required to do so in planning two sample lessons, but, when not specifically required to, most reported not using this model in planning practice teaching lessons. The results of this study contradict the hypothesis that teachers do not use the systematic planning model because they are not well trained in its use or because the organizational environment is not supportive. Novice and experienced teachers alike demonstrated knowledge of the model, and the teaching environment (a mastery learning system) was organizationally supportive of it. Yet the systematic planning model was not the approach of choice for either beginning or experienced teachers.

McLeod (1981) provided a new perspective on the role of learning objectives in planning by asking not *whether* objectives are the starting point for planning but rather *when* teachers think about objectives. Working with 17 kindergarten teachers, McLeod conducted a stimulated recall interview with each teacher, using a videotape of a 20-to 30-minute classroom activity taught by the teacher earlier that same day. The purpose of the interviews was to determine (following Pylypiw, 1974) when teachers formulated intended learning outcomes in terms of four stages:

Preactive Stage 1: Before planning activities or selecting materials

Preactive Stage 2: After planning but before teaching

Interactive Stage 3: During the act of teaching

Postactive Stage 4: During reflection after a teaching episode

The interviews were also used to determine what types of intended learning outcomes (cognitive, social, and psychomotor) teachers formulated at each stage.

Averaging the responses across the 17 teachers, McLeod found that the largest percentage of intended learning outcomes was identified during Interactive Stage 3 (45.8 %). This was followed by Preactive Stage 1 (26.5 %), Preactive Stage 2 (19.5 %), and Postactive Stage 4 (8.2%). The data also indicated that 57.7% of the intended learning outcomes were cognitive, 35% were social or affective, and 7.2% were psychomotor or perceptual. Interestingly, teachers reported identifying social–affective intended learning outcomes primarily during the interactive stage, and cognitive outcomes predominantly during the preactive and postactive stages.

Unfortunately, in her investigation, McLeod relied primarily on stimulated recall interviews. She could have supplemented the stimulated recall data to good effect with classroom observations and with thinking aloud techniques to describe the use of learning outcomes as it was happening. However, this research does much to broaden the concept of goals, objectives, or intended learning outcomes and their roles in planning and teaching. In earlier studies researchers tended to dismiss learning objectives as a rare and, therefore, unimportant element in teacher planning, even characterizing teachers as interested only in activities rather than in outcomes. McLeod's study suggests that teachers can and do think about and act to support both specific and general learning outcomes for their students and that it is hazardous to study the process of teacher planning in isolation from interactive teaching and postactive reflection.

The role of student learning outcomes in planning and teaching has been examined by several other researchers as well (e.g., Connelly, 1972; Eisner, 1967; Eisner & Vallance, 1974; Raths, 1971; Toomey, 1977; and Wise, 1976). The concensus seems to be that planning for teaching necessarily involves the teacher's intentions for learning, but that the degree of specificity and explicitness of these intentions varies with the teacher's conception of the teaching–learning process. Toomey (1977) found, for example, that compared with more process-oriented and student-centered teachers, teachers characterized as content and teacher control oriented tended to be very specific in their articulation of and use of student learning objectives.

Teacher Planning and Teachers' Classroom Behavior

The third and final question concerns the link between teacher planning and action in the classroom. Research has demonstrated that teachers' plans influence the content of instruction and the sequence of topics (e.g., Clark & Elmore, 1981; Smith &

Sendelbach, 1979), as well as the time allocations to elementary school subject matter areas (Smith, 1977). Now we turn to the few studies that have examined how teachers' plans influence what happens in the classroom. Table 3 presents the principal findings of these studies.

Zahorik (1970) compared the effects of structured planning with the absence of structured planning on teachers' classroom behavior. He provided 6 of 12 teachers with a partial lesson plan containing behavioral objectives and a detailed outline of content to be covered 2 weeks hence. He requested that the remaining 6 teachers reserve an hour of instructional time to carry out a task for the researchers, not telling them that they were going to be asked to teach a lesson on credit cards until just before the appointed time. Zahorik analyzed recorded protocols of the 12 lessons focusing on "teacher behavior that is sensitive to students" (p. 144). He defined this behavior as "verbal acts of the teacher that permit, encourage, and develop pupils' ideas, thoughts, and actions" (p. 144). In comparing the protocols of the planners and nonplanners, Zahorik judged that teachers who had been given plans in advance exhibited less honest or authentic use of the pupils' ideas during the lesson. He concluded from this that the linear planning model — goals, activities and their organization, and evaluation — resulted in insensitivity to pupils on the part of the teacher.

Unfortunately, Zahorik did not determine the degree to which the teachers who received the lesson plans in advance actually planned or elaborated the lesson. A competing explanation for these findings is that the teachers who had no advance warning about what they were to teach were forced by the demands of the task to concentrate on their students' ideas and experiences, while those teachers who knew the expected topic of instruction for 2 weeks prior to teaching were influenced to focus on the content rather than on their students.

In the Peterson, Marx, and Clark (1978) laboratory study of teacher planning, teaching, and student achievement described earlier in this chapter, a number of positive relationships emerged between the focus of teachers' planning statements and their classroom behavior. For all teachers, planning on the first of three days of teaching was heavily weighted toward the content to be covered. However, the focus of their planning shifted on Days 2 and 3, with planning for instructional processes becoming more prominent. The proportion of planning state-

Table 3. Four Studies of Links Between Planning and Action: Summary of Findings

Study	Method of Inquiry	Teachers	Subject Matter	Principal Findings
Carnahan (1980)	Analysis of written plans and classroom observation	9 teachers of fifth grade	Mathematics	Positive correlation between planning statements about small-group instruction and observed use of small-group instruction
Hill, Yinger, & Robbins (1981)	Observation, interview, and analysis of written plans	6 teachers of preschool		Planning concerned with selection of materials and arrangement of physical environment of classroom
Peterson, Marx, & Clark (1978)	Think aloud, observation	12 junior high school teachers	Social studies	Positive correlations between focus of planning behavior and focus of interactive teaching behavior
Zahorik (1970)	Classroom observation	12 elementary teachers	Lesson on credit cards	Teachers given plans 2 weeks in advance noted as behaving "less sensitively toward students" than teachers not given plans

ments dealing with the learner was positively related to teacher behaviors classified as "group focused." The proportion of planning statements dealing with the content was positively and significantly correlated with teacher behavior coded as "subject matter focused." These findings suggest that teacher planning was related to the general focus or tone of interactive teaching, rather than to the specific details of verbal behavior. They also suggest that the nature of the work done during the preactive planning period changes with situation-specific teaching experience. As the task demands on the teacher change, so does the nature of appropriate preparation.

Carnahan (1980) studied the planning and subsequent behavior of nine fifth grade teachers while teaching the same 2-week mathematics unit. The quality of the teachers' written plans was determined by rating plans that focused on large groups as low in quality and plans that focused on individuals or small groups as high in quality. (This criterion was chosen because the curriculum materials that the teachers were using incorporated a similar bias.) Classroom observers rated instruction for teacher clarity, use of motivation strategies, and student engagement. The main result of interest here is that Carnahan found no statistically significant relationship between his ratings of plan quality and the ratings of teaching quality. However, he did find a significant positive correlation between the total percentage of written planning statements about small groups or individuals and the observed use of small groups in the classroom. This and other findings in Carnahan's report indicate that the main relationship between written plans and subsequent classroom interaction was in the domain of organization and structuring of teaching rather than in the domain of specific verbal behavior. During interactive teaching, the responses of students are unpredictable and therefore verbal dialogue may not be a profitable focus for teacher planning.

The influence of teacher planning on classroom behavior in the teaching of preschool children seems to be somewhat different from that observed in higher grades. Hill, Yinger, and Robbins (1981) studied the planning of six teachers who constituted the staff of a university developmental preschool. During a 10-week period, the researchers observed the teachers' Friday afternoon group planning sessions, staff meetings, conferences with student teachers, materials selection from the storeroom, and their arranging of their classroom environments. They also interviewed the teachers about their planning processes and copied planning documents and records.

Hill, Yinger, and Robbins found that much of the teachers' planning consisted of selecting and arranging manipulable materials. The school storeroom was an important source of teachers' ideas for learning activities. Once the teachers identified the appropriate materials, they then focused on how to arrange these materials in the classroom for use by the children and on how to manage the transitions into and out of these activities. The teachers spent 3 or more hours per week arranging the physical environments of their classrooms. When an activity did not go well, the teacher's first improvement strategy was to rearrange the physical environment. Because teaching in this setting depended so much on the materials selected and arranged by teachers, teacher planning had a substantial influence on the nature of the children's learning opportunities. Also, the demands of teaching appear to have influenced the nature of the planning process in this setting.

These four studies, taken together, suggest that teacher planning does influence opportunity to learn, content coverage, grouping for instruction, and the general focus of classroom processes. They also highlight the fact that the finer details of classroom teaching (e.g., specific verbal behavior) are unpredictable and therefore not planned. Planning shapes the broad outline of what is possible or likely to occur while teaching and is used to manage transitions from one activity to another. But once interactive teaching begins, the teacher's plan moves to the background and interactive decision making becomes more important.

Summary of Research on Teacher Planning

Research on teacher planning provides a direct view of the cognitive activities of teachers as professionals. This literature is almost exclusively descriptive and deals primarily with the planning of experienced elementary teachers. The research indicates that there are as many as eight different types of planning that teachers engage in during the school year. These types of planning are not independent, but are nested and interact with one another.

The curriculum as published is transformed in the planning process by additions, deletions, changes in sequence and emphasis, teachers' interpretations, and misunderstandings. Other functions of teacher planning include instructional time allocation for subject matters and for individuals and groups of students, study and review of the content of instruction by teachers, organization of daily, weekly, and term schedules, meeting administrative accountability requirements, and communicating with substitute teachers. Teachers also report that the planning process produces immediate psychic rewards in the form of feelings of confidence and reduction of uncertainty. Taken together, these findings suggest that teacher planning has direct connections with variables studied in the general literature of research on teaching such as structuring, opportunity to learn, and time-on-task. Teacher planning also seems to be an appropriate topic of inquiry for researchers studying implementation of educational innovations.

The task of modeling the planning processes of teachers is far from complete. The literature is in reasonable agreement that a narrowly construed version of the linear "rational planning model" does not describe the planning behavior of experienced teachers. But it is not clear whether the several styles and models of planning described by Favor-Lydecker, Toomey, Yinger, and others are functionally superior to the rational model. Furthermore, it may be that training novice teachers in use of a version of the rational model provides them with an appropriate foundation for developing a planning style compatible with their own personal characteristics and with the task environments in which they must teach. Continued study of the planning behavior of teachers might be more profitable if researchers shift to longitudinal designs and a cognitive-developmental framework instead of continuing to accumulate descriptions of the planning of experienced teachers.

Teacher planning reduces but does not eliminate uncertainty about teacher–student interaction. Classroom teaching is a complex social process that regularly includes interruptions, surprises, and digressions. To understand fully the operation of teacher planning, researchers must look beyond the empty classroom and study the ways in which plans shape teacher and student behavior and are communicated, changed, reconstructed, or abandoned in the interactive teaching environment.

It is to teachers' thinking during the process of teaching that we now turn.

Teachers' Interactive Thoughts and Decisions

Researchers on teachers' thinking have attempted to describe the thinking that teachers do while interacting with students in the classroom. More specifically, researchers have been concerned with the extent to which teachers make interactive "decisions" that lead them to change their plans or their behavior in the classroom. For example, while teaching a lesson, a teacher may make a decision to continue with the teaching strategy that he or she had planned to use, or not to continue with the strategy as a result of a decision. Researchers have attempted to "map" the interactive decisions of teachers and describe the influences on teachers' interactive decisions as well as to ascertain the influence on and the cues that the teachers use to make interactive decisions. Finally, researchers have investigated the relationship between teachers' interactive thoughts and decisions, teachers' behavior, and student outcomes. An important question here is whether teachers who are "effective" in producing positive gains in student achievement differ in their patterns of interactive decision making from teachers who are "less effective" in promoting student achievement.

In the following sections, we will review the research on teachers' interactive thoughts and decisions that has addressed each of the above topics. We will discuss findings on the broader topic of the content of teachers' interactive thoughts and then move to a more narrow focus on findings related to teachers' interactive decision making. First, we will provide an overview of the methodology used in these studies.

Overview of Studies Using Stimulated Recall Techniques to Study Teachers' Interactive Thoughts and Decisions

Table 4 presents a summary of the method and procedures of 12 research studies that used stimulated recall interviews to elicit self-reports of teachers' interactive thoughts and decisions.

As can be seen from Table 4, the 12 studies varied considerably in the grade level and experience of the participants; the number and subject matter of the lessons that were videotaped and used in the stimulated recall interview; and the actual format of the stimulated recall interview. Eleven of the 12 studies were done with elementary teachers and students from Grades 1 through 6 while 1 study was done with seventh and eighth grade students. Although most studies included several teachers, each teaching more than one lesson, Wodlinger (1980) focused on only one teacher, and several investigators taped only one lesson for each teacher (Fogarty, Wang, & Creek, 1982; Morine & Vallance, 1975; Semmel, 1977). The subject matter of the lessons that were videotaped varied considerably across the 12 studies and included reading, language arts, spelling, mathematics, social studies, and physical education. To illustrate how the format of the stimulated recall interview differed across the 12 studies, we will describe 1 study and then use it as a basis for comparison.

In a laboratory study of teachers' interactive thoughts and decisions, Peterson, Clark, and Marx (Clark & Peterson, 1981; Marx & Peterson, 1981; Peterson & Clark, 1978) had 12 experienced teachers each teach a $2\frac{1}{2}$-hour social studies lesson to three groups of seventh and eight grade students. Teachers were videotaped while they were teaching. At the end of each lesson, each teacher viewed the videotape of the first 5 minutes of the first hour of teaching and three 1–3 minute segments of each hour of instruction to "stimulate recall" of their interactive thoughts during instruction. After viewing each of these four segments, the teacher responded to the following questions:

1. What were you doing in the segment and why?
2. Were you thinking of any alternative actions or strategies at that time?
3. What were you noticing about the students?
4. How are the students responding?
5. Did any student reactions cause you to act differently than you had planned?
6. Did you have any particular objectives in mind in this segment? If so, what were they?
7. Do you remember any aspects of the situation that might have affected what you did in this segment?

Table 4. Twelve Studies of Teachers' Interactiv‍e

| Study | Participants | | | Number and Typ‍ Lesson Videotap‍ |
	Teachers	Students	Setting	
Colker (1982)	Six experienced first and second grade teachers	Intact classes of the six teachers	Classroom	Three mathemat‍ lessons: one t‍o single student‍ one to a small group; and on‍ a large group
Conners (1978b)	Nine teachers, 1 each from Grades 1, 3, and 6 in three schools in Canada; each with 2 or more years' experience	Intact classes of the nine teachers	Classroom	One 30–60-minu‍ language arts lesson; one 30–60-minute social studies lesson
Fogarty, Wang, & Creek (1982)	Eight teachers from lab school, one preschool, and two experienced first and second grade teachers; four preservice and one experienced third/fourth/fifth grade teachers	Small group of 5–8 students selected from each teacher's intact class	Classroom	One 15-minute lesson (six teachers taugh‍ reading or language arts lesson; one ta‍ mathematics; taught social studies)
Housner & Griffey (1983)	Eight experienced elementary physical education teachers and eight preservice elementary physical education teachers	Four children, ages 7 to 9 years, not previously acquainted with the teachers	Laboratory	Two 24-minute lessons; one o‍ soccer and on‍ basketball dribbling
Lowyck (1980) (Also De Corte & Lowyck, 1980)	16 fifth grade teachers in Belgium	Intact classes of the 16 teachers	Classroom	One mathematic‍ lesson and on‍ geography les‍ topics provide‍ by E. (Same fo‍ teachers)
Marland (1977) (Also Mackay & Marland, 1978)	Six teachers, 1 each from Grades 1, 3, and 6 in two schools in canada	Intact classes of the six teachers	Classroom	One 1-hour language arts lesson and on‍ 1-hour math lesson

Thoughts and Decisions Using Stimulated Recall Interviews

Format of Stimulated Recall Interview

ype of Videotaped nents Used as Stimuli	Type of Interview	Coding and Analysis of Stimulated Recall Interview
re tape viewed vice: teacher stopped pe during first ewing; E stopped pe during second ewing	No questions (only teacher comments) during first viewing; structured questions during second viewing	"Thought units" tallied and categorized
e as Marland, except ' played a more tive role" in lecting segments	Clinical interview with some specified open-ended questions	"Thought units" tallied and categorized; ecological factors and teachers' principles, beliefs, and rules identified and tallied
her viewed entire leotape and stopped when recalling any oughts or decisions; ould also stop tape	Clinical interview with some specifiied "probe" questions	"Decisions" identified; aspects of decisions tallied and categorized
-minute segments of ch lesson selected by perimenter	Structured interview (same questions as Peterson & Clark)	"Decisions" categorized; aspects of decisions tallied and categorized
her viewed entire leotape. (Interview ted 3–5 hours and d not occur on same y as videotaping)	Clinical interview	Content analysis (specific procedures not specified)
her viewed entire leotape and decided en to stop the leotape and reflect thought processes; ould also stop tape	Clinical interview	"Thought units" tallied and categorized; type and aspects of decisions tallied and categorized; "principles of teaching" identified

91

	Participants			
Study	Teachers	Students	Setting	Number and Type Lesson Videotape
McNair (1978–1979)	10 teachers from one school in grades 1–5 with 3 years or more experience	Two intact reading groups (1 more able; 1 less able) in each teacher's class	Classroom	One reading less with each of th two groups th times during t year
Morine & Vallance (1975)	10 "more effective" and 10 "less effective" second grade teachers; 10 "more effective" and 10 "less effective" fifth grade teachers	12 students randomly selected from within each teacher's intact class	Classroom	One 20-minute reading lesson topic and curriculum materials provided by E
Peterson & Clark (1978) (Also Marx & Peterson, 1981; Clark & Peterson, 1981)	12 experienced teachers	Three groups of eight randomly assigned seventh and eighth grade students not previously acquainted with the teachers	Laboratory	One $2\frac{1}{2}$-hour soci studies lesson taught to each the three grou of students; curriculum materials provided by E
Semmel (1977) (Also, Semmel, Brady & Semmel, 1976)	20 preservice special education teachers	One student tutee with a severe reading deficit assigned to each teacher	Classroom	One oral reading lesson was audiotaped
Shroyer (1981)	One female fourth/ fifth grade teacher; one male and one female fifth/sixth grade teacher; each with at least four years' experience	The three teachers' intact classes	Classroom	A 1–2-week mathematics u on rational numbers
Wodlinger (1980)	One female sixth grade teacher in Canada with four years of teaching experience	The teacher's intact class of 26 students	Classroom	10 30–45-minute lessons (1 language arts, mathematics, reading, 2 spel lessons; 1 grou discussion)

Format of Stimulated Recall Interview

Type of Videotaped gments Used as Stimuli	Type of Interview	Coding and Analysis of Stimulated Recall Interview
acher viewed entire videotape and stopped it when he or she "made a decision," experimenter also stopped tape, both systematically and at random	Structured interview	"Thought units" tallied and categorized
me as McNair (1978)	Structured interview (same questions as McNair)	"Decisions" identified and categorized; aspects of decisions tallied and categorized
st 5 minutes of the lesson and three short segments randomly selected by E	Structured interview	"Thought units" tallied and categorized; "Decision paths" identified and categorized
tire tape played back; E stopped tape after each pupil "miscue"	Structured interview	"Statements" tallied and categorized
acher viewed entire tape and stopped tape to reflect on thoughts, feelings, and decisions	Clinical interview (similar to Conners)	"Critical moments" identified, tallied, and categorized
acher viewed entire videotape and provided running account of interactive decisions	Clinical interview with "general" and "focused" questions	Decision-related data categorized into "thought units," "decisions," and aspects of decisions tallied and categorized

In contrast to the previous study and the study by Housner and Griffey (1983), where teachers viewed only selected segments of the videotape of their lessons, teachers viewed the entire videotape in eight studies (Conners, 1978b; Fogarty, Wang, & Creek; 1982; Lowyck, 1980; Marland, 1977; McNair, 1978–1979; Morine & Vallance, 1975; Shroyer, 1981; and Wodlinger, 1980), listened to the entire audiotape of their lesson in one study (Semmel, 1977), and viewed the entire videotaped lesson twice in one study (Colker, 1982). However, even in these studies where the interviewer played the entire tape to the teacher, the procedure differed according to whether the teacher selected the videotaped segments that were the focus of the interview (as in the Lowyck, Wodlinger, & Shroyer studies), whether the teacher and interviewer were both allowed to select segments that were the focus of the interview (as in the Conners, Fogarty et al., Marland, McNair, and Morine & Vallance, studies) or whether the interviewer selected the segments that were the focus of the interview (as in the Semmel & Conners studies). Moreover, in the Peterson, Marx, and Clark study and in the studies by Colker, Housner and Griffey; McNair, Morine and Vallance; and Semmel, teachers responded to a structured interview with a prespecified set of questions. In contrast, in the studies by Conners, Lowyck, Marland, Shroyer, and Wodlinger, the format of the stimulated recall interview was a clinical one in which a few general and specific questions were predetermined by the researchers, but the actual questions varied from interview to interview as determined by the interviewer.

Although the format of the stimulated recall interviews differed considerably across the 12 studies, the coding and analysis of the stimulated recall interviews were similar in all the studies. The teachers' responses to the interview were audiotaped and coded by categorizing each of the teacher's statements or "thoughts" into one of several categories. The number of complete thoughts in each category was then tallied and compared across content categories. We turn now to the findings from these studies.

The Content of Teachers' Interactive Thoughts

Six studies have described the content of teachers' interactive thoughts. These are: Marx and Peterson (1981), McNair

(1978–1979), Colker (1982), Marland (1977); Conners (1978b), and Semmel (1977). Despite the variability in the methodology used in these six studies, the findings from the studies are remarkably similar. Table 5 presents the percentage of teachers' interactive thoughts by content category across the six research studies. In this table, we placed similar categories side by side so as to permit comparison of the percentage of teachers' interactive thoughts in similar categories across studies.

Several findings emerge from an examination of Table 5. First, a relatively small portion of teachers' reports of their interactive thoughts deal with instructional objectives. Teachers mentioned objectives only 14% or less of the time across the four studies that used objectives as a category. Examples of teachers' reports of interactive thoughts about objectives include:

"I wanted them to see the connection between the 'Sh' sound and the S-H, that they all had S-H's on them."
"I wanted them to identify the senses that they were using."

Second, a relatively small percentage of teachers' statements about their interactive thoughts deal with the content or the subject matter (5% to 14% across three studies). An example of such a statement is, "At this point here I wanted to focus in on the idea of Japan being today an industrial nation, rather than an agricultural nation."

Third, a relatively larger percentage of teachers' reports of their interactive thoughts deal with the instructional process including instructional procedures and instructional strategies. The percentage was amazingly similar — 20% to 30% — across the five studies that used a category like "instructional process" in their content analysis. Some examples are:

"I thought after I explained it to her, 'I didn't make that very clear.'"
"I was also thinking that I couldn't ask them to come down to the carpet one group at a time."
"I was thinking that they needed some sort of positive reinforcement."
"At this point in the lesson I felt I had reviewed what we had already talked about yesterday."
"I was trying to guide her into the sounding without actually having to do it."

Table 5. Percentage of Teachers' Interactive Thoughts by Content Category Across Six Research Studies

Marx & Peterson		McNair		Colker		Marland		Conners		Semmel	
Category	%	Category	%	Category	%	Category	%	Category	%	Category	%
Objectives	13.9	Objectives	2.9			Goal statements	2.7	Objectives	5.4		
Content	6.5	Content: facts and ideas	13.6					Content	5.5		
Instructional procedures	30.9	Procedures and task	28.8			Tactical deliberations	23.5	Instructional moves	21.7	Instruction and/or text	19.2
Materials	6.1	Materials	8.8								
Learner	42.2	Learner	39.1	Learner	41.4	[Total learner	50.0]	[Total learner	44.1]	Learner	59.6
		Time	6.6	Other than learner	58.6	Information: pupil	6.8	Information: pupil	9.7		
								Mediation: pupil	1.3		
						Perceptions	15.6	Perceptions	15.8	Reiteration of behavior	21.1
						[about learner] Interpretations	14.4	[about learner]	12.6		
						[about learner] Anticipations	11.9	Interpretations	16.8		
						[about learner] Reflections	11.6	[about learner] Expectations	15.2		
						[about learner]	8.6	[about learner] Self-awareness	4.3		
						[about learner]	18.8		4.3		
						[about learner Information: other]	6.1	[about learner Information: other]	7.7		
						Feelings	5.6	other	1.0		
						Fantasy	0.1	Beliefs	1.0		
								Beliefs	4.4		
								Feelings	6.5		

Fourth, all of the six studies found that the largest percentage of teachers' reports of their interactive thoughts were concerned with the learner. Examples included the following:

"I was thinking that they don't understand what they're doing."
"I was also thinking, 'Tricia's kind of silly right now. If I ask her, I probably won't get a straight answer.'"
"I expected him to get that."
"You can't always tell with kids you know, whether they're truly inattentive or whether they're just mulling over what has been going on."
"... So they were concentrating on that."
"... and nobody was listening at all."

In the studies by Marx and Peterson, McNair, and Colker, the percentage concerned with the learner was approximately 40%. In the study by Semmel (1977), the percentage was higher (60%), perhaps because this was the only study in which teachers were dealing with exceptional children (i.e., children with a severe reading difficulty) or perhaps because in this study each teacher was teaching only one child. In contrast, Colker (1982) found no significant differences between teachers' reports of interactive thoughts about learners in a tutoring situation compared to a small-group situation or a large-group situation. Thus, the greater focus on the learner in the Semmel study is probably due to the fact that the students were exceptional children or possibly to the fact that the teachers were preservice rather than in-service teachers.

In the studies by Marland and Conners, a small percentage of teachers' reports of their interactive thoughts were categorized as "Information: pupil." However, a further analysis of their data shows that a large proportion of teachers' statements about the learner were included in their four categories entitled "perceptions," "interpretations," "anticipations" ("expectations") and "reflections" ("self-awareness"). The percentage dealing with the learner in each of these four categories is indicated in brackets in Table 5. If one adds together the percentages about the learner in each of these four categories with the category of pupil information, then the total percentage of teachers' reports of interactive thoughts dealing with the learner in the Marland study is 50% — a percentage that comes close to the percentages reported in the other four studies. If one conducts the same analysis on the categories in the Conners study, one finds that the total percentage of teachers' statements about the learner including perceptions about the learner, interpretations about the learner, expectations about the learner, self-awareness about the learner, information and mediation about the learner, is 44.1 %.

In sum, then, *in all of the six studies, the greatest percentage of teachers' reports of interactive thoughts were concerned with the learner.* If one looks only at the studies in which normal learners were taught, the percentage of interactive thoughts reported about the learner was between 39 % and 50 %.

While the results in Table 5 present a consistent picture of the percentage of teachers' reports of interactive thoughts that fall into each of several broad categories (i.e., objectives, content, instructional process, and learner), they also suggest that it may be useful to subdivide these categories into more specific categories. In contrast to the categories used by Marx and Peterson (1981) and McNair (1978-1979), Marland's (1977) categories reflect more of a "cognitive processes" description of teachers' interactive thoughts:

Perceptions: Units in which the teacher reported a sensory experience (e.g., one that was seen or heard).

Interpretations: Units in which the teacher attached subjective meaning to this perception.

Anticipations: Speculative thoughts or predictions made interactively about what could, or was likely to, occur in future phases of the lesson.

Reflections: Units in which the teacher was thinking about past aspects of, or events in, the lesson other than what had been done.

Conners (1978b) and Lowyck (1980) used similar categories to describe teachers' interactive thoughts. These categories come closer to describing the *processes* that teachers engage in during teaching, and, as such, move us closer to a cognitive processing analysis of teaching similar to the analyses of human problem solving and decision making that have been conducted by cognitive psychologists (see, for example, Shulman & Elstein, 1975). Moreover, these results suggest that, in the future, researchers might construct a content by processes matrix of teachers' interactive thoughts. The content would reflect *what* the teacher is thinking about during interactive teaching (e.g., objectives, subject matter, instructional process, the learner, materials, or time) and the processes would reflect *how* the teacher is thinking about it (i.e., perceiving, interpreting, anticipating, or reflecting).

All the categories in Table 5 reflect interactive thoughts that are directly related to the teacher's task of teaching. With the possible exception of the category "fantasy," none of the categories suggests that teachers' thoughts ever include "off-task" thoughts such as thoughts about what they are going to do after school, or thoughts about their personal problems or personal life.[1] This is in distinct contrast to the content of students' reports of interactive thoughts during a stimulated recall interview. When students are shown videotaped segments of themselves in a teaching–learning situation, they freely admit to and describe off-task interactive thoughts (see, for example, Peterson, Swing, Braverman, & Buss, 1982; Peterson, Swing, Stark, & Waas, 1983).

Because it seems unlikely that teachers' interactive thoughts are always task relevent, and it seems likely that off-task thoughts would sometimes intrude, then the high frequency of task-relevant thoughts shown in Table 5 may be an artifact of the stimulated recall procedures that were used in these studies. If teachers have control over stopping the videotape and talking about their interactive thoughts, then they are likely to pick only those places where they are having task-relevant interactive thoughts. Moreover, because the interviewers did not convey to the teachers that it was acceptable to have "off-task" thoughts, the demand characteristics of the situation may have been such that the teachers felt obliged to report only interactive thoughts that were "on-task." Thus, teachers may have selectively recalled or reconstructed their reports of their interactive thoughts to reflect only task-relevant thinking.

Teachers' Interactive Decisions: Definition and Frequency

While some researchers have attempted to describe the content of teachers' interactive thoughts, other researchers have attempted to identify teachers' interactive "decisions." The ra-

---

[1] Thanks to Gregory Waas for this observation.

tionale for such a focus on teachers' interactive decision making is best summarized in the following statement by Shavelson (1973):

> Any teaching act is the result of a decision, whether conscious or unconscious, that the teacher makes after the complex cognitive processing of available information. This reasoning leads to the hypothesis that the basic teaching skill is decision making. (p. 18)

The above quote by Shavelson suggests that each action of the teacher is based on an interactive decision by the teacher. However, because of the obvious methodological problems involved in any attempt to "probe the unconscious," most researchers have restricted their definitions and defined teachers' interactive decisions as a "conscious choice" by the teacher during classroom instruction. For example, Sutcliffe and Whitfield (1979) defined a decision as a conscious act that occurs when at least two alternatives are available — the choice to change behavior and the choice not to change behavior.

Similarly, Marland (1977) defined a decision as a conscious choice. However, Marland then used a more restrictive operational definition of an interactive decision. Marland coded a teacher's report of interactive thinking as an "interactive decision" only if it included all of the following: (a) explicit reference to consideration of alternatives, (b) evidence that the teacher made a selection and became committed to one of the alternatives, and (c) evidence that the teacher followed through in the lesson with that choice of alternatives. Marland's category of a "deliberate act" appears to reflect more closely a broader conception of an interactive decision as a conscious choice. Marland categorized a teacher's interactive thoughts as a "deliberate act" whenever a teacher saw the need for some action or response but considered only one course of action or whenever a teacher reported taking a certain course of action and then stated the reason for doing so. Thus, by combining "deliberate acts" with Marland's category of "interactive decisions," we would argue that Marland (1977) and Sutcliffe and Whitfield (1979) appear to be in agreement on what constitutes an interactive decision: a teacher's conscious choice between continuing to behave as before or behaving in a different way.

Moreover, Morine and Vallance (1975), Fogarty, Wang, and Creek (1982), Wodlinger (1980), and Shroyer (1981) also agree with this definition. Morine & Vallance (1975) directed the teachers in their study to identify points on the videotape during the stimulated recall interview where the teacher remembered consciously saying to himself or herself, "Let's see, I think I'd better do *this* now," or "I guess I'll try doing this" (Morine & Vallance, 1975, p. 49). Fogarty et al. (1982) asked the teacher to stop the tape at any point where he or she recalled any thoughts or decisions.

Similarly, Wodlinger (1980) defined an interactive decision as consisting of statements or units in which the teacher's thoughts were focused upon the delivery of instructional material or student learning and in which the teacher mentioned the consideration of choice behavior as in the following:

> They weren't too sure yesterday, and they had problems with this stuff, so (I thought I would go back and ask those particular people, that were having problems yesterday.) So with Laura and Steve, you know, (I specifically asked them a question just to see if they were able to understand them from yesterday.) (p. 282)

To be coded as an interactive decision, Wodlinger indicated that the teacher must have reported a deliberate choice to implement a specific new action.

Shroyer's (1981) category of "elective action" also fits into the above definition of teachers' interactive decisions. Shroyer first identified what she called "student occlusions." She defined a student occlusion as a student difficulty or unexpected student performance in the classroom. She then argued that when confronted with a student occlusion, a teacher elects to respond with some action. She further indicated that her term "elective action" was what she meant by a decision, but that she chose this term as an alternative to "decision" because "decision has traditionally implied the consideration of alternatives, a process for which research on interactive teacher thoughts has found little support" (Shroyer, 1981, p. 10).

These investigators have converged on a definition of an interactive decision as a deliberate choice to implement a specific action. Given this definition then, we can ask the question, "What is the frequency of teachers' reported interactive decisions?" Table 6 presents five studies that report results that address this question. In spite of the variations in methodology employed in these five studies (see Table 4), the findings re-

Table 6. An Analysis Across Five Studies of the Frequency of Teachers' Reported Interactive Decisions

Study	Category Name	Mean Frequency Per Lesson	Average Length of Lesson in Minutes	Estimated Number of Decisions (Acts) Per Minute	Range Across Teachers of Mean Decisions (Acts) Per Lesson	Range of Mean Decisions (Acts) Across Lessons and Teachers
Fogarty, Wang, & Creek (1982)	Interactive decisions	8.4	15	0.56	4 to 11	[a]
Morine & Vallance (1975)	Interactive decisions	11.9	20	0.59	[a]	[a]
Marland (1977)	Total of interactive decisions and deliberate acts	28.3	60	0.47	10 to 36	6 to 43
Wodlinger (1980)	Interactive decisions	24.1	35	0.69	[b]	15 to 33
Shroyer (1981)	Elective actions	22.2	45	0.49	8 to 36	[a]

[a] Information not provided in written report.
[b] N = 1; no range can be computed.

ported in Table 6 are remarkably consistent. Across the studies, the estimated number of interactive decisions made by teachers ranged from .5 to .7 per minute. The results of these studies are consistent in suggesting that, on the average, *teachers make one interactive decision every 2 minutes.* Thus, these data suggest that the decision-making demands of classroom teaching are relatively intense.

Teachers' Consideration of Alternative Courses of Action

The above results on the prevalence of teachers' interactive decisions are in sharp contrast to statements by others, such as MacKay and Marland (1978) and Lowyck (1980), who have indicated that teachers' interactive decision making during instruction does not occur as frequently as was expected. This discrepancy may be due to the fact that, originally, some researchers such as Peterson and Clark (1978) suggested that teachers' decision making during interactive teaching involved teachers' considering two or more alternative courses of action when they observed that the lesson was not going well. This conceptualization followed from Snow's (1972) description of teacher thinking during classroom instruction as a cyclical process of observation of student behavior, followed by a judgement of whether student behavior is within desirable limits, followed, in turn, by a decision to continue the teaching process unchanged or to search memory for alternative teaching behavior that might bring student behavior back within the limits of tolerance. If no alternatives are available in memory, the teacher would continue the classroom behavior as previously; if the search yielded a plausible alternative, the teacher might decide to act on that alternative by changing the course of instruction, or might ignore the alternative and continue as before.

THE PETERSON AND CLARK MODEL

Peterson and Clark (1978) presented a model of this sequence of events. This model of a teacher's decision processes during teaching is presented in Figure 2. In addition, Peterson and Clark (1978) identified four alternative paths through the model. These paths are summarized in Table 7. In Path 1, the teacher judges students' classroom behavior to be within toler-

103

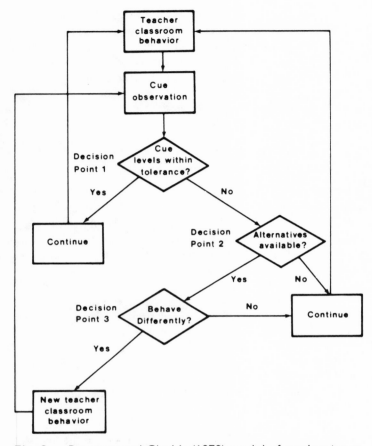

Fig. 2. Peterson and Clark's (1978) model of teacher inter-active decision making.

ance. In other words, the teacher judges that the students are understanding the lesson and are participating appropriately. In Path 2. the teacher judges that students' classroom behavior is not within tolerance. For example, the teacher may judge that the students are either not understanding the lesson or perhaps are being inappropriately disruptive or withdrawn. However, there are no alternative strategies or behaviors in the teacher's behavioral repertoire. In Path 3, the teacher again judges that students' behavior is not within tolerance, and the teacher has alternative strategies or behaviors available in the teaching re-

Table 7   Four Alternative Paths for Teacher Information Processing During Instruction

Decision points	Path 1	Path 2	Path 3	Path 4
Student behavior within tolerance	Yes	No	No	No
Alternatives available?	—	No	Yes	Yes
Behave differently?	—	—	No	Yes

Note. From Peterson & Clark (1978), p.556.

pertoire, but decides not to change teaching behavior to attempt to bring student behavior back within tolerance. Finally, in Path 4, the teacher judges that students' behavior is not within tolerance, but alternative teaching strategies are available, and the teacher decides to behave differently to bring student behavior back within the limits of tolerance.

Peterson and Clark (1978) categorized the reports of the cognitive processes of 12 teachers and found that the greatest majority of teachers' reports of their cognitive processes could be categorized as Path 1. The average proportion of Path 1 ranged from 71% to 61% across the 3 days of teaching. Peterson and Clark argued that because the cyclical repetition of Path 1 represented a teacher's report of conducting "business as usual," it was not surprising that teachers' reports most frequently followed this path. As one teacher put it when he was asked if he was thinking of any alternative actions or strategies, "At this point? No. None at all. It was going along. The only time I think of alternative strategies is when something startling happens" (Peterson & Clark, 1978, p. 561).

Teachers reported considering alternative strategies in only 20% to 30% of the cases across the 3 days of instruction. This latter result is consistent with the findings of other investigators. For example, of the average of 28.3 interactive decisions and deliberate acts reported by the teachers in Marland's (1977) study, only 24% (6.8) of them involved the teacher's explicit reference to considering one or more alternatives and evidence that the teacher followed through with his choice of alternatives.

Some discrepancy exists between the findings of investigators who have attempted to determine *how many* alternative courses of action teachers tend to consider when they consider changing their behavior during interactive teaching. In their study of 18 second grade teachers and 20 fifth grade teachers, Morine and Vallance (1975) found that teachers considered an average of three alternative courses of action. Marland (1977) found that in the vast majority of interactive decisions, teachers reported considering only two alternatives. In his study of one teacher, Wodlinger (1980) found that the teacher considered only one course of action for the majority of her interactive decisions.

These data on the relative infrequency with which teachers consider alternative courses of action during interactive teaching as well as the results which suggest that when teachers do consider alternative courses of action, they do not consider many alternatives, suggest that the model proposed by Peterson and Clark (1978) may not be an accurate reflection of the decision-making processes that teachers engage in during interactive teaching. Shavelson and Stern (1981) proposed an alternative model that was based on the work of Joyce (1978–1979), Peterson and Clark (1978), Shavelson (1976), and Snow (1972). This model is shown in Figure 3.

THE SHAVELSON AND STERN MODEL

Shavelson and Stern based their model on the assumption that teachers' interactive teaching may be characterized as carrying out well-established routines. Research on teacher planning suggests that teachers form a mental image that is activated from memory as a plan for carrying out interactive teaching. (See the section on teacher planning earlier in this chapter for a further discussion of this research.) Shavelson and Stern (1981) argue:

> These images or plans are routinized so that once begun, they typically are played out, much as a computer subroutine is. Routines minimize conscious decision making during interactive teaching and so "activity flow" is maintained. Moreover, from an information-processing perspective, the routinization of behavior makes sense. Routines reduce the information-processing load on the teacher by making the timing and sequencing of activities and students' behavior predictable within an activity flow. (p. 482)

Indeed, the idea that during interactive teaching, teachers follow "routines" did not originate with Shavelson and Stern, but has been suggested by several researchers including Yinger

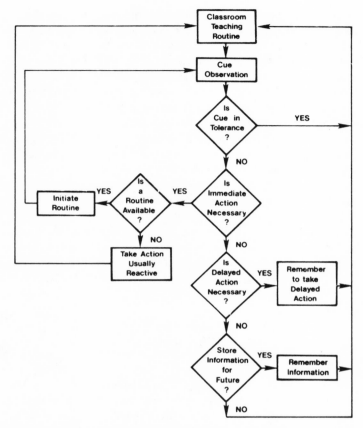

Fig. 3. Shavelson and Stern's (1981) model of teacher inter-active decision making.

(1977), Morine-Dershimer, (1978–1979), and Joyce (1978–1979). Shavelson and Stern's (1981) unique contribution is in presenting a model in which decision making during interactive teaching is portrayed as occurring when the teaching routine is interrupted (see Figure 3). As in the Peterson and Clark (1978) model, the teacher's decision-making process involves the observation of cues and the determination of whether the cues (student behaviors) are within tolerance. However, Shavelson and Stern propose that if student behavior is not within tolerance, the teacher then decides whether immediate action is necessary. If immediate action is necessary, the teacher then decides whether an alternative routine is available and if so to initiate that routine; whether delayed action may be used rather than immediate action; or whether to continue the classroom teaching routine as before.

An advantage of the Shavelson and Stern model is that it incorporates the idea of "routine" as an important concept to explain teachers' interactive teaching behavior and decision making, and it also incorporates the finding that teachers, for the most part, do not consider a large number of alternative courses of action but may consider only one alternative teaching routine as an alternative course of action. But the Shavelson and Stern model, like the Peterson and Clark (1978) model, still assumes that the only antecedent for the teacher's interactive decision is observation of student "cues" and the judgment that students' behavior is not within tolerance. We turn now to research that has investigated the antecedents of teachers' interactive decision making and examined the extent to which observation of student cues serves as the antecedent of teachers' interactive decision making.

Antecedents of Teachers' Interactive Decisions

Marland (1977) investigated the antecedents of teachers' reported interactive decisions. He found that 44% of teachers' reported interactive decisions and deliberate acts occurred in response to a judgment by the teacher that students' behavior was not within tolerance. These indications were (a) student deviance, noise, restlessness, inattentiveness, or disruption (antecedents of 20% of teachers' reported interactive decisions and deliberate acts); (b) incorrect, unsatisfactory, delayed, or incomplete student response or work (antecedents of 19.5% of teachers' reported interactive decisions and deliberate acts); and (c) students' apparent lack of understanding (antecedents of 3% of teachers' reported interactive decisions and deliberate acts).

For the purposes of this discussion, the most important point is that Marland found that the majority of teachers' reported interactive decisions occurred not in response to an observation by the teacher that student behavior was not within tolerance but rather occurred in response to other factors. Teachers reported making interactive decisions in response to a student question or a student-created contact with the teacher (19 % of the reported interactive decisions); when a choice of respondent, participant, or student to be helped was needed (10 % of the decisions); when a choice of appropriate techniques was needed (6 % of the decisions); when there was a transition point in the lesson from one activity to another (8 % of the decisions); when the teacher anticipated a problem or a difficulty (2 % of the decisions); and other miscellaneous factors including insufficient time left in the lesson (5 % of the decisions), shortage of materials (4 % of the decisions) and late arrival of aides (1 % of the decisions). In addition, Marland found that the majority of teachers' reported deliberate acts did not occur in response to student behavior but rather in response to other factors. A large percentage of teachers' reported deliberate acts (29 %) involved the teacher's selection of a student respondent or participant, selection of a specific teaching technique, or selection of appropriate examples in content. Also, a number of deliberate acts occurred in response to a student initiated comment, question, or contact (11 %).

In his study of a single teacher, Wodlinger (1980) also found that 51 % of the teacher's reported interactive decisions had antecedents that originated with the teacher or the environment rather than with the student. Wodlinger reported that 16 % of the teacher's reported interactive decisions originated with the teacher's cognitive state or affective state. This occurred when the teacher's thoughts or feelings were the stimuli for the formulation of an interactive decision. The following excerpt from a stimulated recall protocol illustrates this category of interactive decisions: "*I was mad. I was very cross*, because, um, Michael had lost his math book and ... and I was trying to decide what I was going to do about it, ah, at that point. I thought of some alternatives and thought 'Well, this isn't the time to deal with it,' so I sort of left it" (Wodlinger, 1980, p. 116).

In addition, the environment, including time constraints, interruption by another adult, and instructional material and equipment, served as antecedents for 35 % of the teacher's reported interactive decisions. The antecedents for the remaining reported interactive decisions (49 %) did involve observation of student cues including the teacher's assessments and estimates of student behavior, student cognition, student affect, and other student characteristics, as well as the teacher's judgment of the progress of the lesson and the lesson strategies that she was employing.

Similarly, Fogarty et al. (1982) found that, although cues from students served as antecedents for the majority of teachers' reported interactive decisions (64%), "non-student" cues served as antecedents for a large part of teachers' reported interactive decisions. Finally, although Housner and Griffey (1983) found that teachers' observations of student behavior served as antecedents of 85% of teachers' reported interactive decisions, this uncharacteristically high percentage probably reflects the fact that the stimulated recall interview included a specific question on whether teachers' observations of student behavior caused the teacher to behave differently than planned.

The results of a policy capturing study by Shavelson, Atwood, and Borko (1977) also support the conclusion that factors other than teachers' judgments about students may serve as antecedents for teachers' interactive decisions. Shavelson et al. presented 164 graduate students in education (about two-thirds of them teachers) with a description of a fictitious student named Michael. Sixteen different stories were constructed about Michael and presented to the subjects. These stories contained initial and additional information about Michael which varied in valence (Michael was portrayed as high or low in ability and effort) and in terms of reliability (the information was presented so that one could infer it was either reliable or unreliable). Each subject read only one description of Michael. After reading the description, the subject was asked to make one simulated preinstructional decision and two simulated interactive decisions. The results indicated that when subjects were asked to make an interactive decision that consisted of deciding what they would do if the student failed to answer a question during a mathematics lesson, the subjects considered the information about the student and the ability estimate irrelevant to their interactive decision. A similar picture emerged when the subject was asked to make an interactive decision about reinforcement strategies for Michael. Again, the information about the student presented in the scenario had little effect on the subjects' reported interactive decision. The authors concluded that subjects' interactive decisions depended on information that was not measured in this experiment.

Although the findings from the Shavelson et al. study support the conclusion that factors other than teachers' judgments about students may contribute to teachers' interactive decisions, these results should be interpreted with caution. Subjects' responses to a questionnaire may not bear any resemblence to teachers' interactive decision making during an actual classroom situation. In addition, in simulations of this type, subjects are limited to the information provided (in this case information on the ability and effort of Michael). By limiting the available student "cues" the researchers may have artificially restricted the natural variance in subjects' decisions. (See, e.g., Clark, Yinger, & Wildfong, 1978; Yinger & Clark, 1983.) In addition, the antecedent of a teacher's interactive decision as postulated in the Peterson and Clark model is the teacher's observation of the student's behavior rather than the teacher's judgments of the student's "states of mind" (characteristics such as ability and effort) which were the antecedents that were varied in the Shavelson et al. study. Thus, perhaps if student *behavior* had been varied, then subjects' judgments of student behavior may have affected subjects' reported interactive decisions. This hypothesis is supported by the results of a study by Cone (1978).

In a policy capturing study in which 50 teachers were presented with a description of a fictitious student, Cone (1978) found that the type of deviant student behavior had a significant effect on the teachers' reported managerial decisions. Teachers selected more severe managerial strategies for student behavior that was more severe than for student behavior that was less severe (in order from most severe to less severe: physical aggression, speaking out, out of seat, and noise). However, the way the student was characterized — as having a history of deviancy or as having no history of deviancy — also affected the teachers' reported managerial decisions. Teachers selected more severe managerial strategies for deviant students with a history of deviancy than for students with no history of deviancy. These results confirm that teachers' judgments of student behavior may be an important antecedent of teacher' interactive decisions. However, the question still remains as to why student characteristics were not importantly related to teachers' reported interactive decisions in the Shavelson et al. study, but they were importantly related to teachers' interactive decisions in the Cone study.

A possible explanation is that students' behavior and characteristics are more importantly related to teachers' interactive decisions that are concerned with classroom management than teachers' interactive decisions that are concerned with instruction. In his study of one teacher, Wodlinger (1980) found that students were the antecedents for more of teachers' reported interactive decisions that dealt with classroom management (54%) than teachers' interactive decisions that dealt with instruction (46%). When Wodlinger examined the type of information that the teacher used in making interactive decisions, he found that observed student behavior more frequently served as information used by the teacher in making managerial decisions (34% of the time) than in making instructional decisions (17% of the time).

Toward a New Model of Teacher Interactive Decision Making

Considering the above research findings, we would suggest that neither Peterson and Clark's (1978) nor Shavelson and Stern's (1981) models of interactive decision making are sufficient. Both models need to be revised to reflect two important points. First, a model of teacher interactive decision making should reflect the definition of interactive decision making as a deliberate choice to implement a specific action rather than a choice of actions from several possible alternatives. Second, a model of teacher interactive decision making should reflect the finding that the majority of teachers' reported interactive decisions are preceded by factors other than judgments made about the student. These factors might include judgments about the environment, the teacher's state of mind, or the appropriateness of a particular teaching strategy. Thus, while a large proportion of a teacher's interactive decisions do seem to occur as a result of a teacher's judgment about student behavior, a model that focuses only on student behavior as the antecedent of teacher interactive decisions (as in the Peterson & Clark, and Shavelson & Stern models) does not accurately portray the processes involved in teacher interactive decision making.

Further specification of a model of teachers' interactive decision making requires research on the process whereby a given antecedent condition influences a teacher's interactive decisions. For example, in their models, Peterson and Clark (1978) and Shavelson and Stern (1981) assumed not only that student behavior was the sole antecedent of teachers' interactive decisions, but they also assumed a "threshold" mechanism whereby student behavior affected teachers' interactive decisions. In other words, a teacher was assumed to make an interactive decision only when student behavior was judged by the teacher to be beyond a given "threshold" at which point the teacher judged that student behavior was not within tolerance. Although in proposing their models, these researchers assumed a threshold mechanism whereby student behavior affected teacher interactive decision making, no research has been done to determine whether this is really the case. Research is needed to describe the process whereby a given antecedent condition results in an interactive decision by the teacher. Such studies might employ a process-tracing approach similar to the one used by Yinger (1977) in his study of a teacher's planning throughout a school year. Future models of teachers' interactive decision making also need to take into account the finding by Wodlinger (1980) that more than one antecedent often serves to stimulate the teacher's formulation of an interactive decision.

Specification of models of teacher interactive decision making by Peterson and Clark (1978) and Shavelson and Stern (1981) may have been premature. Calderhead (1981) suggested that such models may be overly constraining. Indeed, we now argue that these models may have led research on interactive decision making in the wrong direction because they assumed that student behavior was the only antecedent condition for teachers' interactive decisions and that teachers consider several possible alternatives, strategies, or courses of action when making an interactive decision. We would suggest, therefore, that before specifying a new model or revising the existing models of teacher interactive decision making, researchers should first do more descriptive research on how teachers make interactive decisions. Specification of a new model of teacher interactive decision making should await the findings from this research. Obviously, such an approach assumes a *descriptive* focus on teacher interactive decision making. At some point, we may want to be *prescriptive*. In other words, researchers may determine that more "effective teachers" are those who focus on student behavior as the primary antecedent condition for making an interactive decision. We turn now to this issue of teacher effectiveness and teacher interactive decision making.

Teacher Effectiveness and Teachers'
Interactive Decision Making

Much research on teaching has been devoted to identifying the behaviors of effective teachers with the intent of using the findings to increase teachers' effectiveness. (See, for example, Brophy & Good, this volume; Dunkin & Biddle, 1974; Peterson & Walberg, 1979). Thus, one might ask the question, "What kinds of interactive decision making do effective teachers engage in?" or, "What constitutes effective interactive decision making by a teacher?" Although, as we shall see, little empirical research has been directed toward answering these questions, several researchers have attempted to conceptualize the interactive decision making of an effective teacher.

Doyle (1979) described an "idealized strategy" for a teacher's information processing. He suggested that at the beginning of the school year, the effective teacher consciously directs attention toward gathering information about a particular classroom group (e.g., the steering group). To gather this information, the teacher implements a limited number of activities that have become "automatized" or routinized for the teacher. Given the routinized nature of these activities, the teacher can then direct "conscious processing" of classroom events toward observing and monitoring "behavior task initiations by students" (e.g., off-task or misbehavior by students). As the students learn the classroom routines, the teacher can introduce more activities that then, in turn, become routinized. Concurrently, the teacher's conscious processing becomes fine tuned and efficient. Eventually all regular activities will be routinized, including administrative operations, recurring lessons, and even instructional moves. The teacher's conscious processing will then be available for specialized purposes such as scanning the room periodically, monitoring particular students or groups of students in the classroom, and solving problems in areas that cannot be routinized. As Doyle (1979) put it,

> In view of the frequency and the cost — in terms of reaction time and consequences of unexpected events, it would seem adaptive and efficient for a teacher to direct conscious processing primarily to discrepancies or anomalies. By specializing in discrepancies, a teacher can anticipate disruptions and reduce the effects of immediacy and unpredictability on task accomplishment. (pp. 62–63)

A similar picture of effective information processing during interactive teaching has been presented by Joyce (1978-1979) and Corno (1981). Corno, for example, argued that effective classroom teachers ought to be consciously engaged in information processing. Teachers should be attending to and observing students' faces, actions, behavior, and voices. They should "see, hear, and then organize and check their perceptions to pace and maintain the flow of instruction and help accomplish instructional objectives" (Corno, 1981, p. 369).

Empirical Research on the Relationship of Teachers' Interactive Decision Making to Student On-Task Behavior and Achievement. Only three empirical studies, Peterson and Clark (1978), Doyle (1977a), and Morine and Vallance (1975), have attempted to describe the thought processes and decisions of effective teachers during interactive teaching. Peterson and Clark (1978) and Morine and Vallance (1975) used the criterion that has been used typically to define effective teachers, namely, students' scores on an achievement test. In contrast, Doyle (1977a) used student classroom behavior as the criterion. He defined successful teachers as those who maintained high levels of student work involvement and low levels of disruptions in their classrooms.

The first study is the one by Peterson and Clark (1978) described previously. Peterson and Clark categorized teachers' reports of their cognitive processes during interactive teaching into one of four paths and then related teachers' scores on the paths to students' achievement scores. (See Figure 9.2 and Table 9.7.) One might argue that a more "effective" path for teacher information processing during instruction would be Path 4, while a less "effective" path for teacher information processing would be Path 3. In other words, one might hypothesize that when effective teachers observe that student behavior during classroom interaction is not within tolerance, they first consider whether alternative teaching strategies or behaviors are available in their repertoire. If so, they then decide to behave differently and to engage in new classroom behavior to bring student behavior back within the level of tolerance. This information-processing path (Path 4) appears to reflect the kind of processing that a successful classroom manager would engage in as indicated by Doyle (1979). Doyle (1979) suggested that the teacher who is a successful classroom manager recognizes "behavior task initiations" (e.g., classroom misbehavior) immediately and intervenes early. This early intervention has the advantage of neutralizing misbehavior before the student's peers in the classroom "reward" the behavior or before public consequences occur. In contrast, failure by the teacher to initiate action that would bring student behavior back within tolerance (Path 3) would define an ineffective classroom manager as described by Doyle and might be considered to constitute ineffective teaching.

In support of the latter conclusion, Peterson and Clark (1978) found that teachers' scores on Path 3 were significantly negatively related to students' achievement scores. Teachers whose reports of information processing during interactive teaching were most often categorized as Path 3 had students who achieved lower scores on a multiple choice achievement test ($r = -.50, p < .05$, one-tailed test) as well as on the factual content of an essay test ($r = -.64, p < .05$, one-tailed test) On the other hand, teachers' scores on the other paths (Path 1, Path 2, or Path 4) were not significantly related to students' achievement scores.

Interestingly, Peterson and Clark (1978) also reported information about the planning of these same teachers. They found a significant positive correlation ($r = .51, p < .05$), one-tailed test) between teachers' planning statements about objectives and scores on Path 3. If a teacher reported having alternative teaching strategies in mind but did not report behaving differently, it may have been because the teacher saw him or herself as pursuing an instructional objective borne in mind as the result of planning. Thus, a teacher's reported decision not to behave differently may have been a logical one based on instructional objectives that the teacher had established during planning. This interpretation is consistent with the findings of a study by Zahorik (1970) in which teachers who had 2 weeks to prepare a lesson were rated as less flexible and more rigid than teachers who had had no opportunity to plan. However, even though the teachers' information processing may have had a logical basis, the present data still indicate that teachers who reported that student behavior was outside tolerance, but who reported that they did not change their behavior, tended to be less effective teachers — to have students who achieved less.

In the second study, Doyle (1977a) observed 58 student teachers for the full duration of their student teaching assignments, which ranged from 8 to 16 weeks. He observed each student teacher for one class period each week. He used an ecological approach in taking field notes and in writing classroom descriptions. The findings showed that, compared to unsuccessful teachers, successful teachers had the following cognitive skills: (a) rapid judgement, (b) chunking, and (c) differentiation. Successful teachers learned to make rapid judgments during interactive teaching. To simplify and deal with the demands created by the complex classroom environment, successful teachers used chunking, or the ability to group discrete events into larger units, and to differentiate or discriminate among units in terms of their immediate and long-term significance.

This definition of "differentiation" is what Corno (1981) referred to as "selectivity." Corno argued that effective teachers engage in the cognitive process of selectivity — separating out important from salient incidental information — during interactive teaching. Similarly, Doyle's categories of chunking and rapid judgment are included in Corno's category of "transformation." Transformation of information involves the processes of comparison, integration, rehearsal, and elaboration. In sum, then, the research findings from the study by Doyle (1977a) confirm the portrayal of the effective teacher as one who engages actively in cognitive processing of information during teaching but who engages in specific kinds of processes, such as chunking and differentiation, which enable the teacher to simplify and make sense of the complex classroom environment.

In support of this latter statement, Morine and Vallance (1975) found that less effective teachers mentioned specific aspects of their decisions more frequently and referred to more items of information that they used in making their decisions than did more effective teachers. In other words, less effective teachers reported having more things in mind as they discussed their interactive decisions during a stimulated recall interview. (See Table 4 for a description of the study and the method.) In this study, more effective teachers were defined as those whose students had higher gain scores on an achievement test, and less effective teachers were defined as those whose students had lower gain scores on an achievement test. Thus, the definition of teacher effectiveness was the one that has been used typically in process–product studies of teaching effectiveness.

Morine and Vallance reported that, compared to teachers with high student achievement gains, teachers with low student achievement gain scores tended to mention a larger number of items that they were taking into account on almost all aspects of interactive decisions that they discussed. This finding might be interpreted to mean that less effective teachers were not engaging as frequently in the cognitive processes mentioned by Corno and Doyle, such as chunking, differentiation, and selectivity, which would enable them to simplify the amount and kind of information that they were taking in during interactive teaching. Perhaps more effective teachers mentioned a smaller number of items because they had successfully "transformed the complexity of the environment into a conceptual system that enabled them to interpret discrete events and to anticipate the direction and flow of classroom activity" (Doyle, 1977a, p. 54). This conclusion is further substantiated by research comparing the interactive decision making of beginning and experienced teachers.

Studies of the Interactive Decision-Making Processes of Beginning versus Experienced Teachers. Calderhead (1981) compared the comments of beginning and experienced teachers in response to descriptions of common classroom critical incidents. Calderhead presented the critical incident orally to the teacher (e.g., "The class is working quietly when a group of children start talking amongst themselves"). He then asked the teacher: "What more do you need to know to make up your mind what to do, and what would you do?" In analyzing experienced and beginning teachers' responses to this task, Calderhead found a marked difference in the nature and sophistication of their interpretations and understanding of classroom events. He found that beginning teachers seemed to either lack the conceptual structures to make sense of classroom events or to have simple undifferentiated structures. Moreover, beginning teachers did not seem to extract the same kind or level of meaning from the description of the critical incident as did experienced teachers.

In recent years, cognitive psychologists have used the word "schema" to describe the way knowledge is stored in memory.

(See, for example, Anderson, 1977, 1984; Nisbett & Ross, 1980; Rumelhart, 1980). As Nisbett and Ross (1980) put it:

> People's generic knowledge also seems to be organized by a variety of ... *schematic*, cognitive structures (for example, the knowledge underlying one's awareness of what happens in a restaurant, one's understanding of the Good Samaritan parable, or one's conception of what an introvert is like). To describe such knowledge structures, psychologists refer to a growing list of items, including "frames," ... "scripts" ... "nuclear scenes" ... and "prototypes" ... in addition to the earlier and more generic term "schemas." (p. 28)

Although Calderhead (1981) did not discuss his findings in terms of experienced teachers having different schemata than beginning teachers, we interpret his results to suggest that experienced teachers may have better developed knowledge structures or "schemata" for phenomena related to classroom learning and teaching than do novice teachers. Similarly, we infer from the findings of Doyle (1977a) and Morine and Vallance (1975) that effective teachers may also have better developed schemata for classroom events than do ineffective teachers. Some relevant schemata for teachers might include (a) knowledge underlying their conception of what schoolchildren are like; and (b) knowledge underlying their awareness of what happens in classrooms.

Interestingly, the findings from a study by Calderhead (1983) indicate that the schemata that experienced teachers have for "schoolchildren" or "students" may differ significantly from the schemata that beginning teachers have for school children or students. Calderhead (1983) used interviews, the repertory grid technique, and stimulated recall to study the perceptions of six experienced teachers, six student teachers, and six teachers who were in their first year of teaching. He found that experienced teachers appeared to have amassed a large quantity of knowledge about children in general. As Calderhead put it, "experienced teachers in a sense 'know' their new class even before they meet them" (Calderhead, 1983, p. 5). Calderhead reported that experienced teachers knew the kinds of home backgrounds of students. They had an idea of the range of knowledge and skills to expect in their class and of the likely number of children who would need special help. They knew the types of misbehaviors and discipline problems that would occur. They knew the kinds of experiences that students tended to have had prior to school and the kinds of activities that the children engaged in outside of school.

Differences between experienced and novice teachers in another kind of schema — knowledge underlying their awareness of what happens in classrooms — may lead experienced and novice teachers to focus on different types of student cues in their interactive decision making. For example, Housner and Griffey (1983) found that while negative cues from students frequently resulted in both experienced and novice teachers' reported decisions to change their behavior (about 45 % of the time), positive student cues resulted more often in experienced teachers' decisions to change their behavior than in novice teachers' decisions to change their behavior (30 % and 6 % of the time for experienced and novice teachers, respectively). With remarkable similarity, Fogarty et al. (1982) found that, of all the cues that led to their interactive decisions, novice teachers reported focusing on students' disruptive behavior most frequently (27 % of the cues reported). In contrast, experienced teachers reported disruptive behavior infrequently in their reports of cues that led them to make interactive decisions (6 % of the cues reported). These results suggest that experienced and novice teachers may differ considerably in their perceptions of classroom events as well as in their underlying schema for what constitutes an "appropriate" flow of classroom events.

Cognitive psychologists have argued that schemata affect perception, understanding, remembering, learning, and problem solving. One can well imagine that the experienced teacher would have better developed schemata as well as schemata more relevant to the teaching situation than would beginning teachers. Similarly, the schemata of "effective teachers" might differ significantly from the schemata of "ineffective" teachers. Presumably, having an appropriate schema for the conception of what a fourth grade child is like as well as an appropriate schema for events and life in a fourth grade classroom would be particularly important and useful if one were a fourth grade teacher. Such schemata would obviously affect the teacher's perception of events during interactive teaching, affect the teacher's perception of the students, enhance the teacher's understanding of events that may occur during interactive teaching, and aid the teacher in problem solving and decision making during interactive teaching.

Training Teachers in Effective Interactive Decision Making

Peterson and Clark (1978), Doyle (1977a), and Morine and Vallance (1975) investigated the relationship between variables related to teachers' interactive decision making and a criterion variable of effective teaching, such as student achievement or students' on-task behavior in class. Similarly, Calderhead's (1981, 1983) studies were descriptive studies. Thus, these studies fall within the correlational part of the correlational–experimental loop that has served as the basis for classroom research following the process–product paradigm (Rosenshine & Furst, 1973). The purpose of correlational research is to identify teaching behaviors that can then be manipulated or trained in experimental studies to determine if training teachers to engage in these "effective" behaviors leads to an increase in student achievement.

Unfortunately, no experimental studies have been undertaken in which researchers have attempted to train teachers in interactive decision-making skills and then to evaluate systematically the effects of training on students' achievement. Although some researchers have attempted to train teachers in effective decision-making skills, these researchers have not systematically evaluated the effects of training on students' achievement. For example, Bishop and Whitfield (1972) created "critical incidents" that could serve as simulation exercises for preservice teachers to practice interactive decision making. They proposed that preservice teachers should read the critical incident and then should be encouraged to develop decision-making skills by asking themselves the following questions: (a) What is the cause of the critical incident? (b) What decision areas are involved in the critical incident (e.g., cognitive learning, affective learning, pupil–teacher relationships, teacher–adult relationships, apparatus and aides, organization and administration)? (c) What criteria should be applied in making the decision? (d) What options are available? (e) Do I have enough information? (f) What is my decision? and (g) How would I evaluate my decision? Although the above model for training teachers in interactive decision making was proposed by Bishop and Whitfield in 1972, Sutcliffe and Whitfield (1979) noted that the technique had yet to be applied widely and evaluated systematically in teacher training. However, Sutcliffe and Whitfield argued that educators should train teachers in interactive decision making and, concurrently, they should evaluate the effects of training on teacher effectiveness, including the effects of training on student achievement gains.

Although we would agree that, eventually, researchers should conduct such experimental studies, we would argue that training teachers in a particular model of interactive decision making is premature. From the correlational research, we have gleaned the notion that *ineffective* teachers' interactive decision making *may* involve (a) the teacher's cognitively processing too great a variety and a quantity of information during the ongoing classroom interaction, without simplifying the information through processes such as chunking and differentiation so that the information can be used effectively in interactive decision making; and (b) a teacher's decision not to change behavior when student behavior is judged to be unacceptable, even though the teacher believes that alternative behavior or strategies are available that could change the student's behavior.

We do not have a clear idea, however, of what constitutes *effective* interactive decision making by a teacher. The teachers who in the Peterson and Clark (1978) study reported following the path that, on the face of it, would appear to be the most appropriate and effective path for a teacher's interactive decision making were not significantly more or less effective teachers than teachers who did not report following this path. On the other hand, if we can believe the findings regarding effective teachers as being better at simplifying, differentiating, and transforming the information perceived during classroom interaction, then perhaps we should focus our experimental research not on training teachers in interactive decision making but rather on training teachers to perceive, analyze, and transform their perceptions of the classroom in ways similar to those used by effective teachers.

Teachers' Theories and Beliefs

Nisbett and Ross (1980) have suggested "that people's understanding of the rapid flow of continuing social events" often depends on their "rich store of general knowledge of objects, people, events, and their characteristic relationships" (p. 28). Nisbett and Ross indicated further that some of this knowledge is organized in schematic, cognitive structures while other knowledge is represented as *beliefs* or *theories*, "that is, reasonably explicit 'propositions' about the characteristics of objects or object classes" (p. 28).

As a person whose daily task is to understand and interpret the rapid flow of social events in a classroom, the teacher obviously relies on these same kinds of knowledge structures that have been described by Nisbett and Ross (1980). We have already described how the first kind of knowledge structures or schemata may affect teachers' information processing and behavior during planning and during classroom interaction. In this section we will discuss the second kind of knowledge, propositional knowledge, that is represented as teachers' theories or beliefs.

Teachers' Theories and Beliefs About Students: Teachers' Attributions for the Causes of a Student's Performance

Psychologists have argued that the types of theories that have the most significant and far-reaching consequences are those theories of a person that focus on the general causes of human behavior (see for example, Heider, 1958; Nisbett & Ross, 1980; and Weiner, 1974). Similarly, in considering teachers' theories and beliefs about students, some researchers have suggested that the most important beliefs that teachers have about students are those that deal with teachers' perceptions of the causes of students' behavior or, in other words, teachers' attributions for the causes of students' performance. (See, for example, Darley & Fazio, 1980; Peterson and Barger, 1984). Indeed, Darley and Fazio (1980) and Peterson and Barger (1984) have suggested that teachers' attributions for the causes of students' performance may be important in attempting to understand how teacher expectancies effect student achievement in the classroom. For these reasons, in our discussion of teachers' theories and beliefs about the student, we will focus on teachers' attributions.

Although the reasearch literature on teachers' attributions is large, we will confine our review to research that addresses four major questions: (a) How have researchers conceptualized teachers' attributions for the causes of students' successes and failures? (b) What factors affect teachers' attributions for the causes of students' performance? (c) What is the relationship between teachers' attributions for the causes of students' performance and teachers' behavior toward these students in the classroom? and (d) What is the relationship between teachers' attributions for the causes of students' performance, teachers' planning and interactive decision making, and students' achievement? (See Peterson and Barger, 1984 for a more complete discussion of the research on teachers' attributions.)

RESEARCHERS' CONCEPTUALIZATIONS
OF ATTRIBUTIONS FOR THE
CAUSES OF STUDENTS' PERFORMANCE

Researchers have differed significantly in the category systems that they have used to describe teachers' attributions for the causes of students' performance. Table 8 presents four alternative category systems that have been used to describe and categorize attributions. Weiner et al. (1971), Frieze (1976), and Bar-Tal and Darom (1979) developed their categories originally to describe students' attributions for the causes of their performance. However, these categories have been used subsequently by other researchers to describe teachers' attributions. In contrast, Cooper and Burger (1980) developed their categories using teachers rather than students as respondents, and they developed the categories explicitly to describe teachers' attributions for the causes of students' performance.

The four category systems in Table 8 also differ to the extent that they were generated a priori by the investigator or generated by the investigator in an attempt to categorize attributions that were provided by subjects in a free-response situation. Weiner et al. (1971) suggested that their experimenter-generated categories were the most common and general of the perceived causes for successes and failures. Frieze (1976) asked 51 college students to explain their own and others' successes and failures on academic and nonacademic tasks. She derived her coding scheme from the college students' open-ended responses. Bar-Tal and Darom (1979) asked 63 fifth grade students to provide explanations for their own grade that they

Table 8. A Summary of Categories Used by Researchers to Describe Students' and Teachers' Attributions for the Causes of Students' Successes and Failures

Weiner et al.'s (1971) Categories	Frieze's (1976) Categories	Bar-Tal & Darom's (1979) Categories	Cooper & Burger's (1980) Categories
Ability	Ability	Ability	Ability (academic, physical, or emotional)
Effort	Stable effort	Effort during test	Previous experience
Task difficulty	Immediate effort	Preparation at home	Acquired characteristics (habits, attitudes, self-perceptions)
Luck	Task	Interest in the subject matter	Typical effort
	Other person	Difficulty of test	Interest in the subject matter
	Mood	Difficulty of material	Immediate effort
	Luck	Conditions in the home	Attention
	Other	Teacher	Teacher (quality and kind of instruction, directions)
			Task
			Other students
			Family
			Physiological processes (mood, maturity, health)

Note. Adapted from Cooper & Burger (1980).

had just received on a test. They then categorized the students' attributions for the causes of their performance into the eight categories shown in Table 8. Cooper and Burger (1980) asked 39 elementary and secondary teachers to list three students in their class that they expected to do well academically and three that they expected to do poorly. They then asked the teachers to list why the outcome was predicted for each student. Cooper and Burger derived their categories from the teachers' free responses.

Most researchers on teachers' attributions have tended to use some subset of the categories presented in Table 8 or some paraphrasing or adaptation of these categories. In addition, researchers have been concerned with some larger, more encompassing dimensions of attributions, such as whether the attribution is to a cause internal to the student (e.g., effort or ability) or external to the student (e.g., luck, task difficulty, or the teacher); whether the attribution is to a stable cause (e.g., ability, task difficulty, or typical effort) or to an unstable cause (e.g., luck or immediate effort). Furthermore, as we shall see, researchers have been concerned with whether teachers tend to attribute students' successes and failures to themselves (i.e., the teacher) and thereby take responsibility for students' performance, or whether they tend to attribute students' performance to factors other than the teacher (e.g., students' effort, ability), thereby eschewing responsibility for the students' performance. An implicit assumption of researchers has been that if teachers fail to accept responsibility for students' successes or failures, and thus fail to see a relationship between their behavior and students' performance, they would be less likely to work to improve these students' performance in the classroom. Thus, researchers have been concerned with factors that affect teachers' attributions and, in particular, the extent to which teachers accept responsibility for students' successes or failures.

FACTORS THAT AFFECT TEACHERS' ATTRIBUTIONS: THE SELF-SERVING BIAS

Attribution theorists have hypothesized that a person's causal attributions will be affected by whether the person is an actor in the situation (i.e., one of the participants in the social interaction) or an observer (i.e., an onlooker who is uninvolved in the social interaction). (See, for example Jones & Nisbett, 1971.)

Because teachers are active participants in the classroom interaction process that leads to students' successes and failures, teachers' attributions for the performance of students might be affected by or biased systematically by their role as an actor rather than as an observer. The teacher's role as an actor may lead to two different patterns of teachers' attributions: (a) ego-enhancing attributions, or (b) counter-defensive attributions. Ego-enhancing or self-serving attributions occur when, as a result of being a participant in the social interaction, teachers attribute a student's successful performance to themselves as teachers and a student's failure to factors other than the teacher. Teachers thereby enhance their egos by accepting responsibility for students' successes while blaming the students for their failures. In contrast, counter-defensive attributions occur when the teacher accepts responsibility for students' failures and gives credit to the students themselves for successes.

Research findings have been inconsistent in indicating the extent to which being an actor in the situation leads the teacher to form ego-enhancing attributions for the student's performance. Table 9.9 presents the findings from this research. Four studies have found that being an actor in the situation leads the teacher to form ego-enhancing attributions (Beckman, 1970; Brandt, Hayden, & Brophy, 1975; Johnson, Feigenbaum, & Weiby, 1964; and Wiley & Eskilson, 1978). In contrast, three studies found support for a counterdefensive bias in teachers' attributions (Ames, 1975; Beckman, 1973; and Ross, Bierbrauer, & Polly, 1974). Peterson and Barger (1984) suggested that the results of these seven studies are not necessarily inconsistent and may be interpreted as indicating that teachers are less likely to make ego-enhancing attributions in more naturalistic situations. They argued that in contrast to the previous experimental studies by Johnson et al. (1964), Beckman (1970), and Beckman (1973), the studies by Ross et al. (1974) and Ames (1975) were more ecologically valid because the researchers employed an actual student confederate and permitted the "teacher" to interact during teaching with the "student." The findings of these latter two studies imply that in actual classroom settings, teachers would be more likely to make counterdefensive than ego-enhancing attributions for the causes of students' performance.

Why might teachers in an actual classroom setting be more likely to make counterdefensive attributions than self-serving

Table 9. Studies Investigating the "Self-Serving" Bias in Teachers' Attributions (Ego-Enhancing Attributions)

Study	Subjects	Task	Results
Ames (1975)	Undergraduate students in educational psychology	Teaching a concept classification task to a 10-year-old male confederate in one 15-minute session	"Teachers" attributed students' failure significantly more often to themselves than to the student or the situation; they attributed students' successes significantly more often to the students themselves. (nondefensive attribution.)
Beckman (1970)	Preservice teachers were the "teachers"; undergraduate psychology students were the "observers"	Teaching mathematics to two fictitious elementary schoolchildren	"Teachers" attributed a student's successful performance to themselves as teachers and a student's failure to factors other than the teacher (i.e., characteristics of student or situation). (Ego-enhancing attributions.) "Observers" attributions were not affected by student performance.
Beckman (1973)	Preservice and in-service teachers assigned randomly to be either "teacher" or "observer"	Teaching mathematics to a fictitious fifth grade student	"Teachers" attributed any change in student's performance to themselves (i.e., counterdefensive attributions) more often than did "observers."
Beckman (1976)	49 parents and 9 teachers of fourth, fifth, and sixth grade students (40% were from minority groups)	Attributions given by teachers for high-, medium-, low-performing students in their classes; parents rated their children on attributions for performance	On open-ended questions, parents of successful students were more likely to mention teaching than teachers. (Teachers never mentioned teaching as a factor on open-ended questions.) On structured questions, parents attributed performance at all levels to teacher factors as often as to child factors (ability and effort), while teachers attributed performance more often to child factors than to their own teaching.

Study	Subjects	Task	Findings
Brandt, Hayden, & Brophy (1975)	Undergraduate students in introductory psychology	Teaching government to a fictitious fourth grade student in 4-minute lectures	"Teachers" who taught successful students assigned more responsibility to themselves (rather than to the student) than did teachers who taught unsuccessful students. (Ego-enhancing or self-serving attributions.)
Johnson, Feigenbaum, & Weiby (1964)	Preservice teachers enrolled in educational psychology course	Teaching mathematics to two fictitious fourth grade boys	Teachers attributed an improvement in students' performance to themselves as teachers; they attributed a lack of improvement to the students themselves. (Ego-enhancing attributions.)
Ross, Bierbrauer, & Polly (1974)	Preservice and in-service teachers were "teachers"; undergraduates were "teachers" or "observers"	Teaching spelling to a sixth grade confederate of the experimenter	"Teachers" attributed students' failure more often to themselves than to the student and attributed students' success more often to the students than to the teacher; this effect was more pronounced for actual teachers than for undergraduate "teachers." (Nondefensive attributions.) Undergraduate "observers" and "teachers" did not differ significantly in their attributions.
Tetlock (1980)	Undergraduate students in introductory psychology served as "observers"	Reading simulated materials from the Ross et al. study (including teachers' attributions which were varied systematically) and rating the teachers	Hypothesis was that teachers' counterdefensive (nondefensive) attributions are "self presentations" designed to create favorable impressions in others. Consistent with this hypothesis, observers rated moderately counterdefensive teachers (those in the Ross study) as significantly more competent than the moderately or highly defensive (ego-enhancing) teacher.
Wiley & Eskilson (1978)	126 elementary school teachers	Completing questionnaire after reviewing the file of a fictitious student who varied in sex, race, and past performance	Teachers were rated as playing a more important role in successful performance of a student than in unsuccessful performance. (ego-enhancing attributions.)

attributions? Tetlock's (1980) results support the hypothesis that teachers' counterdefensive attributions are "self presentations" designed to create favorable impressions in others. (See Table 9.). In an actual classroom setting,, teachers would be likely to be concerned about the impressions that they are making on persons that they come into contact with on a daily and regular basis including students, parents, fellow teachers, and the principal. Thus, teachers would tend to make counterdefensive attributions to enhance their perceived competence. Thus, in the end, teachers' counterdefensive attributions may also be self-serving.

As an extension of this argument, Peterson and Barger (1984) proposed that in a naturalistic classroom setting teachers might even show a "humility bias" in their attributions. In the only study to date in which teachers' attributions for the cause of the performance of actual students in their own classroom were compared with parents' attributions for the same children, Beckman (1976) found that, on open-ended questions, teachers *never* mentioned teaching or the teacher as a factor determining a student's performance (see Table 9.). Perhaps in a situation in which teachers know their students well and in which they are concerned about creating a favorable impression (in this case, with the experimenters who would read their responses and the parents of the students who also provided attributions for the cause of their child's performance), teachers may not take credit for their students' performance because they do not want to appear arrogant. A desire to create a favorable impression may have led to a "humility bias" in teachers' attributions.

Ames (1982) proposed an alternative explanation for the inconsistent findings regarding the self-serving bias in teachers' attributions. Ames proposed that teachers' attributions were affected by an additional factor — teachers' "value for responsibility." He hypothesized that a teacher's value for responsibility involves three key beliefs: (a) that teaching is an important activity, (b) that teachers engage in intentional acts to produce positive outcomes, and (c) that students' success is generally feasible given the situation and constraints. Ames predicted that high-value teachers (i.e., teachers who placed a high value on teaching) would take responsibility for their own actions and for the performance of their students (i.e., attribute students' performance and their own performance to the teacher). In contrast, Ames predicted that low-value teachers (i.e., teachers who placed a low value on teaching) would attribute students' performance to the students themselves or to situational factors. Ames did note one exception. He hypothesized that high-value teachers would attribute a successful student performance to the student because this attribution was logically consistent with the belief that good teachers reinforce their students for success to encourage the student to work hard.

Although Ames' (1982) hypotheses are appealing intuitively, little research has been done to test whether teachers' value for responsibility does indeed affect teachers' attributions. Ames (1982) reported the results of two studies that supported the hypothesized relationship between teachers' value for responsibility and teachers' attributions. However, in both these studies the findings were based on questionnaire responses from college instructors, and the obtained response rate was extremely low in both studies (39% in the first study and 31% in the second study). Because of this low response rate, the results may not be representative; in particular, the results may be biased if, in fact, only those instructors who placed a high value on teaching (the topic of the questionnaire) were the ones who returned their questionnaires. Thus, although Ames' results are provocative, more research is needed that explores the relationship between the value that teachers place on teaching and their attributions for students' performance in the classroom.

OTHER FACTORS THAT AFFECT TEACHERS' ATTRIBUTIONS

In addition to the teacher's role in classroom interaction, researchers have hypothesized that other factors also affect teachers' attributions for the causes of students' performance. These factors include the teacher's perception of students' past performances as well as characteristics of the students, including race, social class, and sex.

Peterson and Barger (1984) concluded that research findings show that teachers use information about a student's past performance in making attributions about the causes of the student's present performance so as to maintain a "consistent" picture. Teachers are likely to attribute an "expected" outcome, such as success by a student perceived as high in ability, to a stable factor such as ability. On the other hand, teachers are likely to attribute an "unexpected" outcome, such as success by a student perceived as low in ability, to an unstable factor such as luck. One insidious outcome of this impression-maintenance attribution bias is that even students who work hard to dispel a teacher's misconception of their lack of ability might not receive full credit from the teacher for their actions.

The effects of race and social class on teachers' attributions are less clear. Researchers have hypothesized that teachers perceive that black students have less control over their successes and failures than white students and that black students' failures are due to bad luck rather than lack of ability. Findings by Wiley and Eskilson (1978) supported this hypothesis. Cooper, Baron, and Low (1975) showed that the effect of race on teachers' attributions was mediated by students' social class. In addition, Domingo-Llacuna (1976) and Feuquay (1979) found that the effects of race on social class were more complex when teachers' internal and external attributions for students of different races were broken down into specific attributions, such as ability, effort, and luck for the causes of students' successes and failures.

In contrast to the findings for race and social class, sex of student has not been shown to be a significant factor affecting teachers' attributions. For example, Wiley and Eskilson (1978) found that sex of the stimulus student in a description provided to teachers had no significant effect on the causal attributions that teachers made for students' performance. Similar nonsignificant effects of sex were reported by Hanes (1979). On the other hand, Dweck, Davidson, Nelson, and Enna (1978) reported significant sex differences in the attributional statements that teachers made to girls and boys in their classrooms. Teachers were more likely to make statements attributing failure to a lack of effort for boys than for girls. However, studies by Blumenfeld, Hamilton, Wessels, and Falkner (1977) and Heller and Parsons (1981) have failed to replicate the Dweck et al. (1978) findings.

THE RELATIONSHIP BETWEEN TEACHERS' ATTRIBUTIONS AND TEACHERS' BEHAVIOR

Attribution theorists have stated that a significant relationship exists between a teacher's attributions for the causes of a student's performance and the feedback that the teacher gives to the student. In an initial study, Weiner and Kukla (1970) found that the greater the student's success, the more positive the teacher's feedback. Students who were perceived by the teacher as expending effort were rewarded more and punished less than students who were perceived as not trying. Perceived effort was a far more important determinant of reward and punishment than perceived ability.

Most research on the relationship between teachers' attributions and their behavior has tended to support the conclusion that teachers' attributions to effort are highly predictive of the teachers' feedback to the student. Research in support of this conclusion includes studies by Cooper and Burger (1980), Covington, Spratt, and Omelich (1980), Medway (1979), Meyer (1979), Silverstein (1978). The only contrary evidence has been reported by Cooper and Baron (1977, 1979). Table 10. summarizes the results of the studies. Peterson and Barger (1984) concluded that the majority of the evidence suggests that students who are perceived by teachers as expending effort (i.e., teachers attribute their performance to effort) are rewarded more and punished less by teachers than students who are perceived as not really trying. (See Peterson and Barger, 1984, for a more complete discussion of the results.) They also suggested that teachers' affect or emotion may serve as a mediator between teachers' attributions and behavior. In support of this position, Prawat, Byers, and Anderson (1983) found that teachers were angry when they perceived that a student had failed due to lack of effort.

Although the majority of the research has examined the relationship between teachers' attributions and teacher feedback, two studies have explored the possibility that teachers' attributions may affect other kinds of teacher behavior. The results of a study by King (1980) suggest that teachers' attributions for the causes of a students' performance may affect the number and kind of interactions that the teacher has with the student. (See Table 10.) Brophy and Rohrkemper (1981) reported that teacher attributions for a student's performance affected the types of goals that the teacher sets for the student, the way in which the teacher controlled and managed the student's behavior, and the type of educational practices that the teacher used with the student. While these latter findings are suggestive rather than conclusive, they do indicate teacher behaviors that might be investigated in future studies of the relationship between teachers' attributions and teachers' behavior.

Table 10. Studies on the Relationship Between Teachers' Attributions and Teacher Behavior

Study	Subjects	Task	Results
Cooper & Baron (1977)	Eight elementary teachers	Nine target students were selected for whom the teachers had high, medium, or low expectations, respectively. Teachers were asked to assign responsibility for each student's performance to (a) personal or (b) environmental factors. Target student–teacher behavior was observed. Response to Meyer (1979).	Perceived responsibility for success did not predict teacher praise; perceived responsibility for failure did not predict teacher criticism. As perceived responsibility for success increased, number of negative behavior interactions decreased and frequency of child-created interactions decreased; as perceived responsibility for failure increased so did child-created procedural interactions. Performance expectations were more potent predictors of teachers' feedback than were teachers' attributions.
Cooper & Baron (1979)			(a) Effort and ability are not orthogonal in real life—they covary; (b) laboratory studies such as those done by Meyer and attribution theorists show different results than those using face-to-face interaction; (c) Meyer's own data show that low ability attributions resulted in *less*, not more reward.
Cooper & Burger (1980)	62 preservice teachers	A questionnaire was read in which a successful or unsuccessful student was described, with 12 causal attributions for student's performance. For each attribution teachers stated how strongly they would praise/criticize the student and whether they would work more/less with the student.	Teachers showed a greater intention to criticize failure when it was due to internal, unstable, nonteacher causes (i.e., attention, physiological processes, immediate effort). Failure caused by external events (task, teacher, other students, family) led to the *least* intention to criticize. Greater intention to praise success existed when caused by teacher influence (i.e., attention, immediate effort, interest, teacher) than when caused by little influence (i.e., psychological processes, family, other students, task).
Covington, Spratt, & Omelich (1980)	364 students enrolled in introductory psychology; half were randomly assigned to the "teacher" condition	A questionnaire described eight failure situations in terms of overall effort (high or low), stability of effort expenditure (stable or unstable) and direction of unstable low effort. "Teachers" dispersed feedback to	Low student effort, regardless of stability, led to more negative teacher feedback than did high effort. Low-effort pupils were seen by teachers as less conscientious, less motivated, less persistent, more likely to procrastinate, and lazier. Indeed, punishment did not depend on teacher inferences about student ability but on motivational labeling. (Findings support Meyer, 1979.)

(continued)	...two "successful" students, and two "unsuccessful" students in the class (case study)	...and news with and observations of students and the teacher were presented.	Student A (success attributed to ability by the teacher) was often called on by the teacher when she wanted to change pace or direction of lesson. Student B (success attributed to effort) was believed by teacher to "catch on" with merest clues. When student requested help, the teacher expected the problem to be minor. Student C (lack of success due to lack of ability) was provided additional academic support by teacher—helped her understand task requirements and worked through a problem with her. Teacher frequently interacted with Student C. Student D (lack of success due to lack of effort) was seldom interacted with by the teacher.
Medway (1979)	24 elementary teachers who had each referred a child for special education	Teachers were asked to rate the importance of each of the following factors in contributing to the student's major problems: ability; effort; adjustment or personality; home situation; educational preparation; teaching. Teachers were observed interacting with the target children. Criticism of Cooper and Baron (1977).	Teachers' effort attributions were the only attributions that significantly predicted teacher's use of criticism (accounting for 32% of the overall 63% variability in teacher criticism predicted). Teachers gave more criticism to students whose performance was attributed to low versus high effort. Teachers' attributions were not related to teachers' use of praise.
Meyer (1979)			The personal responsibility measure used by Cooper and Baron was criticized for not looking specifically at ability versus effort. Attribution studies have shown that outcomes attributed to high effort receive more praise than low effort. Attributions to low ability receive more praise than attributions to high ability. Meyer also presented his own data which showed a significant positive relationship between effort and teacher reward while the relationship between ability and teacher reward varied according to ability–effort correlation.
Silverstein (1978)	96 teachers in Grades 1–12	Evaluation was made of 24 fictitious students who varied in situational dimensions, ability, effort, and outcome (within-SS design).	Significant main effect of effort was found with greater effort being evaluated more positively, regardless of ability or outcome.

For the most part, research on teachers' attributions has pro-
ceeded separately from research on teacher planning and
teachers' interactive thoughts and decisions. Virtually no over-
lap exists between the names of researchers whose research we
described above in the sections on teachers' planning and interactive decision making and the names of researchers who have
conducted research on teachers' attributions. Even though
teachers' attributions were mentioned early on as an important
topic to be considered in research on teachers' thought processes (see, for example, National Institute of Education,
1975a), this research has not been integrated into the ongoing
body of research on teachers' thought processes. It is not surprising, therefore, that we found no studies that investigated the
relationship between teachers' attributions and teachers' planning or between teachers' attributions and teachers' interactive
thoughts and decisions. Presumably, the effect of teachers' attribution on teachers' behavior would be mediated through
teachers' thought processes either prior to instruction (e.g.,
teacher planning) or during instruction (e.g., teachers' interactive thoughts and decisions). Thus, the link between teachers'
attributions and teachers' preactive and interactive thoughts
and decisions remains an important one that needs to be examined.

A similar problem exists with regard to the relationship
between teachers' attributions and student achievement. Although researchers on teachers' attributions have assumed implicitly that teachers' attributions for the causes of students'
performance have subsequent effects on students' performance
and achievement, they have not explicitly studied the relationship between teachers' attributions and student achievement.
Similarly, researchers on teaching effectiveness, who have been
concerned primarily with effects of teaching on student achievement, have tended not to focus on teachers' attributions although they have considered the potential effects of teachers'
expectations on student achievement. (See, for example,
Brophy, 1982.)

In sum, although teachers' attributions are obviously central
to an understanding of the mental life of teachers, research is
needed that explicates the relationship between teachers' attri-

butions for the causes of students' performance and teachers' preactive and interactive thoughts and decision. In addition, research is needed that moves from laboratory settings in which researchers employ questionnaire and simulation methods to study teachers' attributions to real-world classroom settings in which researchers study teachers' attributions as part of the teachers' ongoing thoughts and actions during everyday teaching. In these settings, researchers also need to investigate the relationship between teachers' actual attributions for the causes of students' performance, teachers' thoughts and behavior, and students' classroom performance and achievement. Only then will we have a better understanding of the importance of teachers' beliefs about students, as represented by their attributions for the causes of students' performance.

Teachers' Implicit Theories of Teaching and Learning

Research on teachers' implicit theories constitutes the smallest and youngest part of the literature of research on teacher thinking. Yet, according to Munby (1982), inquiry into this topic is central to a complete and useful understanding of thought processes in teaching. While we may learn much that is interesting and useful from a technical point of view from research on teacher planning, interactive thinking, and teachers' attributions, we can make sense of these findings only in relation to the psychological context in which the teacher plans and decides. For an individual teacher, this psychological context is thought to be composed of a mixture of only partially articulated theories, beliefs, and values about his or her role and about the dynamics of teaching and learning. The purpose of research on teachers' implicit theories is to make explicit and visible the frames of reference through which individual teachers perceive and process information.

Studies of teachers' implicit theories are difficult to summarize briefly. Reports of several of the studies have been published as books or reported in lengthy doctoral dissertations. Thus, our condensation of this research is necessarily selective and incomplete in its details, and might best be used as an annotated index and guide to this literature rather than as an exhaustive summary and review.

As is the case with much of teacher thinking literature, the studies of teachers' implicit theories are small-sample descriptive research. The nine studies summarized in Table 11 constitute those that focus on teachers' implicit theories directly. The methods of inquiry included ethnographic participant observation, clinical interviews, stimulated recall, and the repertory grid technique. The terms used to designate the topic of study included the teacher's personal perspective (Janesick, 1977), conceptual system (Duffy, 1977), principles of practice (Marland, 1977), construct system (Bussis, Chittenden, & Amarel, 1976), practical knowledge (Elbaz, 1981), and implicit theories (National Institute of Education, 1975b). Although each of these terms has a somewhat different meaning, they hold in common the idea that a teacher's cognitive and other behaviors are guided by and make sense in relation to a personally held system of beliefs, values, and principles. Prior to the researcher's intervention, these systems are typically not well specified, and the central task of the researcher is to assist the teacher in moving from an implicitly held and private belief system to an explicit description of his or her cognitive frame of reference. Because much of this domain is unexplored territory, a great deal of energy has gone into inventing and discovering appropriate language to describe teachers' implicit theories in ways that remain faithful to the teachers' own felt sense of what they believe.

Some researchers have focused on teachers' implicit theories about a particular part of the curriculum (e.g., Duffy's 1977 work on conceptions of reading). Other researchers have been concerned with teachers' general conceptions of their role (Janesick, 1977; Munby, 1983), with their beliefs about curriculum (Bussis et al., 1976), and with the principles that they use to explain their own interactive behavior (Conners, 1978b; Marland, 1977). Elbaz (1981) was more concerned with discovering the structure and content of teachers' practical knowledge than with describing the particulars of the knowledge held and used by one teacher. Ignatovich, Cusick, and Ray (1979) provide us with a striking picture of the conflicting belief systems about teaching held by teachers and administrators.

TEACHERS' PERSPECTIVES OF THEIR ROLES AS TEACHERS

In a 7-month-long ethnographic field study of a sixth grade teacher and his class, Janesick (1977) attempted to discover and describe the perpsective held by that teacher about his role.

Taking a symbolic interactionist view, Janesick defined a perspective as a reflective, socially derived interpretation of experience that serves as a basis for subsequent action. The teacher's perspective combines beliefs, intentions, interpretations, and behavior that interact continually and are modified by social interaction. At any given time, teachers' perspective serves as the frame of reference within which they make sense of and interpret experience, and act rationally.

Janesick found that the broadest and most dominant aspect of the teacher's perspective was his commitment to creating and maintaining a stable and cohesive classroom group. The teacher made plans and interactive decisions and interpreted classroom events in terms of their impact on the group cohesiveness of the class. He defined the most important aspect of his teaching role as that of group leader. Group consensus and cooperation were his main criteria for a successful classroom activity.

TEACHERS' CONCEPTIONS OF READING

A study by Duffy (1977) of teachers' conceptions of reading differed from Janesick's work in several ways. Rather than building a picture of one teacher's conceptions inductively, as Janesick did, Duffy began with a typology consisting of five contrasting approaches to the teaching of reading, derived from literature review: basal text, linear skills, natural language, interest, and integrated whole. A sixth conceptual system labeled "confused/frustrated" was added later. The purposes of the Duffy study were to describe the distribution of these conceptions of the teaching of reading among teachers and, in a second phase of the study, to compare teachers' espoused beliefs with their actual classroom behavior.

Duffy had 350 teachers of beginning reading sort propositional statements about the reading process into five categories ranging from "most like me" to "least like me." Each of the six conceptions of reading listed above was represented by 6 propositions, giving a total of 36 propositional statements to be sorted. Only 37 of the 350 teachers were found to manifest strong "pure types" of conceptions of reading. This finding suggests that perhaps the conceptions that teachers do hold about the teaching of reading do not fit neatly into the research-based typology and that they may be more complex and eclectic than those of reading researchers.

Table 11. Nine Studies of Teachers' Implicit Theories

Study	Method of Inquiry	Teachers	Findings
Bussis, Chittenden, & Amarel (1976)	Clinical interview	60 elementary teachers implementing open or informal teaching	Four contrasting orientations identified for each of four aspects of teachers' belief systems: (a) curriculum priorities, (b) role of children's needs and feelings, (c) children's interests and freedom of choice, and (d) importance of social interaction among children.

Conners (1978b)	Stimulated recall	Nine elementary teachers; 1 each from first, third and sixth grades in three schools	1. Three overarching principles of practice:
			  a. Suppressing emotion
			  b. Teacher authenticity
			  c. Self-monitoring
			2. Five general pedagogical principles:
			  a. Cognitive linking
			  b. Integration
			  c. Closure
			  d. General involvement
			  e. Equality of treatment

Duffy (1977)	Repertory grid technique and observation	Eight teachers of beginning reading	Four of eight teachers behaved in ways consistent with their espoused belief systems about teaching reading. The teaching behavior of the remaining four teachers departed, to various degrees, from their espoused beliefs.

Elbaz (1981)	Clinical interview and observation	One teacher of high school English	1. Five content areas of teacher practical knowledge:
			  a. Curriculum
			  b. Subject matter
			  c. Instruction
			  d. Milieu
			  e. Self
			2. Five orientations of practical knowledge:
			  a. Situational
			  b. Social
			  c. Personal
			  d. Experiential
			  e. Theoretical

Study	Method	Sample	Results

			3. Three structural forms of practical knowledge:
			  a. Rules of practice
			  b. Practical principles
			  c. Images

Ignatovich, Cusick, & Ray (1979)	Q-sort	47 elementary teachers, 22 elementary principals, and 12 administrators	1. Teachers and principals had similar belief systems regarding effective teaching that stressed the humanistic, social, and group process aspects of the teacher's role. 2. Administrators implementing "rational management systems" defined effective teaching in terms of standardized test results, administrative evaluation, and the influence of outside forces on classrooms.
Janesick (1977)	Participant observation	One teacher of sixth grade	Teacher's perspective centrally concerned with creating and maintaining a stable and cohesive group.
Marland (1977)	Stimulated recall	Six elementary school teachers; language arts and math lessons by two first grade and two third grade teachers; language arts lessons only by two sixth grade teachers	Five principles of practice documented: 1. Compensation 2. Strategic leniency 3. Power sharing 4. Progressive checking 5. Suppressing emotions

Munby (1983)	Repertory grid technique	14 teachers of junior high school	1. Wide individual differences in teachers' role definitions linked to variations in curriculum implementation.
			2. The number of constructs needed to describe a teacher's implicit theory ranged from three to six.
			3. Five most common constructs in teachers' implicit theories:
			  a. Student learning and developmental goals
			  b. Student involvement
			  c. Teacher control and authority
			  d. Student needs and limitations
			  e. Motivation

Olson (1981)	Repertory grid technique and interviews	Eight teachers of science in three British comprehensive secondary schools	1. High teacher classroom influence and control was the primary construct around which teachers' theories of good teaching were organized. 2. Teachers transformed and distorted new curriculum to fit their implicit theories of teaching.

In the second phase of the Duffy study, the 37 teachers who manifested strong unitary conceptions of reading completed a modified version of the Kelly Role Repertory Test to refine further and specify more clearly their beliefs about reading. Eight teachers from this group who continued to manifest clear and categorical conceptions of reading were each observed teaching reading in their own classrooms on 10 occasions. The extent to which these teachers' instructional behavior reflected their expressed conceptions of reading was determined by analysis of ethnographic field notes and postobservation interview data. Duffy (1977) reported:

> Four teachers consistently employed practices which directly reflected their beliefs; these included two teachers who had structured beliefs (basal/linear skills), a teacher who had an eclectic view, and one of the teachers having an unstructured belief system (natural language/interest/integrated whole). Of those whose practices did not reflect their beliefs, two of the teachers having strong unstructured belief systems were found to be smuggling elements of unstructured practices into an administratively-imposed program reflecting a structured view. Two other teachers holding unstructured views, however, did not consistently reflect their beliefs; one of the teachers employed practices which, to a large degree, were counter to the unstructured belief system she espoused, while a second teacher operationalized unstructured beliefs only some of the time with some pupils and some activities. (pp. 7–8)

The Duffy study of conceptions of reading portrays a flexible and complex relationship between teachers' implicit theories and their classroom behavior. The results suggest that constraints on teacher behavior such as mandated curriculum materials, resources, time available, habits, and student abilities may interpose between theory and action and account for observed discrepancies. Because the study design began with researcher-selected categories of conceptions of reading that described only about 10% of the teachers surveyed, the results speak as much to what teachers' conceptions of reading are not as to what they are.

TEACHERS' IMPLICIT THEORIES AND BELIEFS IN OPEN EDUCATION SETTINGS

Bussis et al. (1976) described teachers' understandings of curriculum, learners, and their working environments through use of extensive clinical interviews of 60 elementary school teachers who were attempting to implement open or informal instruction. Transcripts of the interviews were coded using a coding system devised by the researchers. The Bussis et al. description of the teachers' "curriculum construct systems" revealed a tension between the press to emphasize grade-level facts and skills and the need to work toward broader developmental and process goals for learners. The researchers identified four orientations among these teachers ranging from heavy and exclusive emphasis on grade-level facts and skills to primary emphasis on broader developmental goals. The teachers' orientations concerning students' emotional needs and feelings ranged from the position that the needs and feelings of students were relatively unimportant or irrelevant as a teaching priority (20% of the teachers) to the belief that the expression of needs and feelings was integral to and inseparable from the learning process (33%). Similarly wide variance was found in teachers' beliefs about the importance of students' interests, freedom of choice in what and how they learn, and about the role of social interaction among children as a means to learning. (See Clark & Yinger, 1977, for a more extensive account of the results of the study.)

Bussis et al. moved beyond the a priori category system approach of Duffy to a coding approach derived from teachers' responses to clinical interviews. The results highlight the wide variations in teachers' belief systems even within a sample of teachers who shared a commitment to open education and informal learning.

PRINCIPLES OF PRACTICE

Two doctoral dissertations completed at the University of Alberta (Conners, 1978b; Marland, 1977), although primarily concerned with the thoughts of teachers during the interactive teaching process, also revealed much of interest about the principles that guide and explain teacher behavior. One of Marland's analyses of stimulated recall interview transcripts permitted him to derive five principles of practice that were mentioned independently by at least two of the six teachers studied or that played a powerful role in influencing the interactive behavior of one teacher. These principles of practice can be described as follows:

The principle of compensation represented an attempt on the part of the teacher to discriminate in favor of the shy, the introverted, the low-ability group, and the culturally impoverished. Two of the four teachers who applied this principle were Grade 1 teachers. This principle figured less prominently in the explanations of teachers of higher grades.

The principle of strategic leniency was a variation of the principle of compensation. Strategic leniency referred to a teacher's tendency to ignore infractions of classroom rules by children who the teacher regarded as needing special attention.

The principle of power sharing involved the teacher using the informal peer power structure to influence students. In this way, the teacher was seen as sharing both responsibility and authority with certain students. That is, the teacher would selectively reinforce the good behavior of students whom she perceived as class leaders to use their influence on their peers as an instrument for classroom management.

The principle of progressive checking involved periodically checking progress, identification of problems, and providing encouragement for low-ability-group students during seatwork. In addition to the direct assistance provided during this checking, the teacher who utilized this principle also reasoned that she was providing stimulus variation for students with short attention spans.

The principle of suppressing emotions was derived from teacher reports that they consciously suppressed the emotional feelings that they were experiencing while teaching. This principle was invoked because of the belief that, if they expressed their feelings and emotions, it might overly excite the students and encourage them to express their own feelings and emotions, thus creating a management problem.

The five principles of practice identified by Marland seem to deal primarily with student characteristics. Compensation, strategic leniency, and power sharing all require that the teacher know his or her students well enough to judge which children would benefit from the kinds of selective responses indicated by each principle. Suppressing emotions is a preventative strategy involving teacher self-management for the sake of orderly classroom management. By implication, teachers who use this principle believe that their students are emotionally volatile and that expression of emotions by students is inappropriate and constitutes a breakdown of class management. Progressive checking is, in part, a straightforward strategy for dealing with the task demands of seatwork. But the teachers also explained their instructional management behavior in terms of its appropriateness as a treatment for children with short attention spans. In Marland's analysis, conceptions of knowledge or conceptions of a particular subject matter are conspicuously absent among principles guiding interactive teacher behavior.

Conners (1978b) replicated and extended Marland's results with nine elementary teachers. His analysis of stimulated recall protocols revealed that all nine teachers used three overarching principles of practice to guide and explain their interactive teaching behavior: suppressing emotions, teacher authenticity, and self-monitoring.

The principle of suppressing emotions was similar to that described by Marland. But in addition to its use as a disruption-prevention strategy, Conners' teachers reported using what could be called "visible suppression of emotions" (e.g., remaining silent and stern-faced until the class quiets down), and also intentionally violating this principle by occasionally expressing anger or frustration to make a powerful impression on their students. This last example suggests that principles of practice can be used flexibly by teachers and even appropriately contravened in certain circumstances.

The principle of teacher authenticity involved teacher presentation of self in such a way that good personal relationships with students and a socially constructive classroom atmosphere would result. This principle was expressed as a desire to behave in ways that were open. sincere, honest, and fallible.

The principle of self-monitoring was defined as the need for teachers to remain aware of their behavior and the estimated effects of their behavior on their students. For the teachers interviewed by Connors, this principle seemed to be acted upon at a global and intuitive level of judgment, for example, by asking oneself "How am I doing ?" regularly during teaching.

Conners also identified five general pedagogical principles held by teachers: cognitive linking, integration, closure, general involvement, and equality of teatment. The first two of these principles dealt with how information to be learned should be organized and presented.

The principle of cognitive linking dictated that new information should be explicitly related by the teacher to past and future student learning experiences. *The principal of integration* called for opportunities for students to practice and apply skills and concepts learned in one subject area in other subjects and contexts in pursuit of transfer of training. *The principle of closure* involved teacher commitment to the importance of summarizing, reviewing, and tying together main points at the end of a lesson or unit. Taken together, these three principles imply a view of the student as an active learner who stores and retrieves information on the basis of meaningful connections among facts and concepts and for whom transfer and integration require explicit practice.

The final two principles claimed by Connors' teachers dealt with their commitments regarding the social dynamics and ideology of the classroom. *The principle of general involvement* was expressed as the desire to have all students participate fully in class activities, to minimize student isolation (self-selected or otherwise), and to help shy or withdrawn students to overcome their reluctance to participate. *The principle of equality of treatment* called for fair and consistent treatment of each student. It is possible to imagine classroom situations in which these last two principles would conflict, for example, violating the principle of equality of treatment to provide special attention, encouragement, or reward to withdrawn students for their full participation in a learning activity. This hypothetical example suggests that principles of practice, while useful as general guides for planning, organizing, and teaching in the classroom, are not sufficient by themselves and require artful interpretation, balance, compromise, and, occasionally, intentional violation to serve the experienced teacher well.

Elbaz (1981) examined the practical knowledge of one high school English teacher who was also developing a course on learning skills at the time of the study. Elbaz reports the particulars of this teacher's practical knowledge in great detail in her doctoral dissertation (Elbaz, 1980, 1983). For the purposes of this review, the most relevant findings of this study concern the nature of teacher practical knowledge, as summarized in Table 11. The five content areas of teacher practical knowledge (curriculum, subject matter, instruction, milieu, and self) are largely self-explanatory and not at all surprising. The five orientations of practical knowledge claimed by Elbaz (situational, social, personal, experiential, and theoretical), taken together, suggest that a teacher's practical knowledge is not acquired vicariously and abstractly (as in a teacher preparation course) but is learned, tested, and developed through field experience.

The three structural forms that Elbaz uses to describe teacher practical knowledge (rules of practice, practical principles, and images) provide a particularly useful framework for thinking about the research on teachers' implicit theories and about the dynamics of those theories in use. According to Elbaz, rules of practice are brief, clearly formulated statements prescribing how to behave in frequently encountered teaching situations. Implementation of a rule of practice is a simple matter of recognizing a situation and remembering the rule. In contrast, a principle of practice is a more general construct than a rule of practice, derived from personal experience, and embodying purpose in a deliberate and reflective way, which can be drawn upon to guide a teacher's actions and explain the reasons for those actions. The use of a principle of practice depends largely on teacher reflection. Thirdly, images are personally held mental pictures of how good teaching should look and feel, expressed by the teacher in terms of brief metaphoric statements or analogies. According to Elbaz, teachers work intuitively rather than analytically to realize their images of good teaching.

TEACHERS' IMPLICIT THEORIES VERSUS CURRICULUM DEVELOPERS' THEORIES.

Two related studies of teachers' implicit theories took as their starting point the problem of implementation of new curricula. Both studies employed a version of the repertory grid technique to elicit labels for constructs that the teachers used in thinking about, evaluating, and classifying teacher and student behavior. In both studies each teacher's own words were used, in large measure, to describe his or her implicit theory of teaching. In the first study, Olson (1980, 1981) presented a list of 20 teaching events, selected to reflect a wide range of science teaching methods, to eight science teachers who were implementing a new curriculum in British secondary schools. Each teacher was asked to sort and group the 20 statements, to discuss the basis for grouping with the investigator, and then to coin a label for each group. These labels were termed "constructs" by Olson. Finally, the teacher-generated construct labels (plus five construct labels supplied by Olson) were arrayed along the horizontal axis of a grid, with the 20 statements about teaching and learning arrayed along the vertical axis. Each teacher then noted the degree of relationship between each construct and each teaching–learning statement. The results of this rating process were used to describe relationships among constructs through correlational analysis and among statements about teaching and learning through factor analysis.

Olson determined that, for these teachers, the most important underlying construct in their implicit theories of teaching was classroom influence. The new science curriculum being implemented at the time of the study called for reduced teacher influence in the classroom "as a consequence of project features such as: free ranging discussion episodes; downplaying in the design the importance of content in science teaching and examination preparation; requiring teachers to instruct outside their discipline" (Olson, 1981, p. 265). According to Olson's (1981) analysis, the teachers dealt with the tension between their belief that teacher influence should be high and the curriculum developers' belief that teacher influence should be low by "domesticating" the curriculum project so that it became compatible with the teachers' implicit theories of good teaching:

> For example: discussions became lectures or recitations; intellectual skills development was translated as content memorization and examination rehearsal; the integrated design was translated as a patchwork of specialized content to be unravelled and resewn; criterion referenced assessment was translated as norm based. In short, after a period of experimentation during which they saw their influence declining, the teachers re-established influence through varied domestications of the project doctrine. (p. 265)

In a related study of the implicit theories of teaching of 14 teachers of junior high school, Munby (1983) used the repertory grid technique in two sessions, separated by 3 days. In the first session, the investigator asked each teacher to generate a set of brief statements describing what one might see during a visit to one of the teacher's classes. After generating about 20 descriptive statements (called "elements" by Munby), each teacher was asked to group the cards on which the statements were written into as many groups as made sense to the teacher. Next, each teacher was asked to discuss the bases for groupings and the distinction and other relationships between groups of statements. The investigator recorded the terms and phrases used by each teacher to explain and rationalize the groupings, and these became the "constructs" constituting the teacher's implicit theory. Finally, the "elements" and "constructs" were listed along the two axes of a grid, and the teacher was asked to consider each element in turn and rate the strength of its association with each construct.

Between the first and second interviews, Munby factor-analyzed the grid to produce construct groupings. The purpose of the second interview was to discover what beliefs and principles underlie the resultant factors. This interview and analysis process produced labels for each of the factors and teacher explanations of the relationships between the factors. From the transcripts of these second interviews, Munby identified a set of teacher statements that constituted the principles and beliefs that he characterizes as "phrases, statements, or terms which convey significant meaning to the teachers and to us about their professional activity" (Munby, 1983, p. 27).

Munby makes a forceful case that the most appropriate mode for reporting findings from his research is the case study. His report offers excerpts from 14 case studies that illustrate the wide individual differences in the implicit theories of teachers working at the same school and even within the same subject matter specializations. The existence of these idiosyncratic variations in beliefs and principles is used by Munby to explain how and why a nominally common curriculum is inevitably interpreted and implemented differently by each teacher teaching from it. In describing the general nature of teachers' implicit theories as derived from this study, Munby found that each teacher enunciated between three and six principles. The five most frequently mentioned construct categories were (a) student learning and developmental goals, (b) student involvement, (c) teacher control and authority, (d) student needs and limitations, and (e) motivation.

The Olson and Munby studies provide a sense of both the variability and consequentiality of teachers' implicit theories about teaching. Both researchers make a persuasive case for staying close to the language of practice in eliciting and describing teachers' belief systems, a position also supported by Elliott (1976). When implementing a significant curricular, organizational, or instructional change, these researchers argue that teachers' belief systems can be ignored only at the innovator's peril. These findings are supported by the results of a Q-sort study by Ignatovich et al. (1979), in which the belief systems of elementary teachers, elementary principals, and of those administrators attempting to influence classroom procedures by implementing rational management models were contrasted. They found that both teachers and elementary principals' belief systems emphasized positive relations between teachers and students, a constructive classroom social system, and humanistic approaches to instruction. In contrast, "rational management system" administrators defined effective instruction in terms of student achievement on standardized tests, abstract models of classroom learning, administrative evaluation, and the influence of outside forces on classrooms.

SUMMARY

It is difficult to synthesize a clear and unequivocal set of conclusions about teachers' implicit theories from this small and eclectic collection of studies. At the very least, we can say that teachers do seem to hold implicit theories about their work and that these conceptual systems can be made more explicit through a variety of direct and indirect inquiry techniques. Even within what appear to be relatively homogeneous groups of teachers (e.g., teachers implementing open education approaches) there is wide variation in the content and orientation of teachers' implicit theories. The several studies that describe teachers' principles of practice suggest that relatively few such principles (three to six) are needed to describe a teacher's implicit theory of teaching.

The principles of practice that teachers draw upon to explain their interactive teaching behavior deal (directly or indirectly) with student characteristics and states, teacher states, and, to a lesser extent, with the structure and organization of subject matter. Duffy's (1977) study of conceptions of reading suggests that the correspondence between teachers' espoused beliefs and classroom behavior is not always high and is moderated by circumstances that are beyond the teacher's control. This study also signaled a gradual move away from the language of researchers and toward the language of teachers in describing teachers' implicit theories.

The Ignatovich et al. (1979), Olson (1981), and Munby (1983) studies raise the possibility that conflict between teachers' implicit theories about good teaching with those of administrators or curriculum developers may explain historic and continuing difficulties in implementation of educational innovations.

Elbaz's (1981) analysis of teachers' practical knowledge, especially concerning the three structural forms of practical knowledge, holds promise as an organizing conceptual system for future research and modeling of teachers' implicit theories and belief systems in use.

Conclusions

The *Second Handbook of Research on Teaching* (Travers, 1973) did not include a chapter or even a reference to research on teachers' thought processes. The research reviewed in this chapter and the view of teaching and inquiry that guide this research are new. Many of these studies raise as many questions as they answer, about method as well as about teachers' thought processes. These limitations notwithstanding, however, our review suggests a number of broad conclusions about research on teachers' thought processes.

First, the research shows that thinking plays an important part in teaching, and that the image of a teacher as a reflective professional, proposed originally by the NIE Panel 6 on Teaching as Clinical Information Processing (National Institute of Education, 1975a), is not far fetched. Teachers do plan in a rich variety of ways, and these plans have real consequences in the classroom. Teachers do have thoughts and make decisions frequently (one every 2 minutes) during interactive teaching. Teachers do have theories and belief systems that influence their perceptions, plans, and actions. This literature has given us an opportunity to broaden our appreciation for what teaching is by adding rich descriptions of the mental activities of teachers to the existing body of work that describes the visible behavior of teachers.

Because this research is so new, each study seems to break new ground. At this time, we have little that could be called a systematic and cumulative body of research. Most of the research on teachers' thought processes has been done with teachers of elementary school, and there is a conspicuous absence of attention to the thought processes of secondary school teachers. Researchers have also tended to focus on relatively discrete and isolated aspects of teachers' thoughts and actions, rather than on the whole process of teaching or on the relationships between, for example, teacher planning and interactive thoughts and action in the classroom. While a narrow focus may be useful early in a research enterprise, the time seems right for more comprehensive study of the full variety of teachers' thought processes in relationship to teachers' actions and their effects on students. Similarly, a vast majority of teachers participating in this research have been experienced teachers. The literature provides us with little sense of how teacher planning, interactive thinking and decision making, and implicit theories and beliefs develop over time, and, therefore, what kinds of interventions might help these processes along. Longitudinal studies of the development of teachers' thought processes would be one answer to this need.

The many different contexts in which these studies of teacher thinking have been done highlights the variety of task demands encountered in teaching. Teachers' thought processes seem to constitute a more or less adaptive array of responses to perceived task demands of the profession. This literature provides a reasonably good start at describing teachers' cognitive behavior, but has not done an adequate job of describing the tasks and teaching situations that call for thoughtful teaching. Researchers would do well to work simultaneously on descriptive models of teacher thought processes and on descriptive models of the tasks of teaching.

While research on teachers' thought processes is new, it has deep roots in early teaching effectiveness and curriculum research. Studies of teacher thinking are potential sources of hypotheses about and explanation of some of the puzzling and contradictory findings of process-product research on teaching and of curriculum change implementation research. For example, if teachers' implicit theory about learners or their mental image of effective teaching were contrary to that embodied in a new curriculum or an experimental teaching method, they would be unlikely to bring the innovation alive with great enthusiasm, thoroughness, and persistence. Alternatively, if an innovation or experimental treatment were introduced after a teacher's yearly and term planning were complete, it would be unlikely that the innovation would be integrated into the classroom activity flow as thoroughly as the researcher would hope. Teacher thinking, as represented in this literature, can be thought of as a set of moderating contextual factors that could influence substantially the outcomes of teacher effectiveness and curriculum effectiveness studies.

While no single study has documented every aspect of the thought processes of a teacher, from this literature we can elaborate on the picture of the teacher as a reflective and thoughtful professional that was sketched out by NIE Panel 6 (National Institute of Education, 1975a). The emerging picture of the teacher as a reflective professional is a developmental one that begins during undergraduate teacher education (or even earlier) and continues to grow and change with professional experience. The teacher education majors who would become professionals in this sense are firmly grounded in the disciplines and subject matters that they will teach. Their study of subject matter focuses on both content and on the cognitive organization of that content in ways useful to themselves and to their future students. They have had both supervised practice in using the behavioral skills and strategies of teaching and have also been initiated into the less visible aspects of teaching, including the full variety of types of planning and interactive decision making. The maturing professional teacher is one who has taken some steps toward making explicit his or her implicit theories and beliefs about learners, curriculum, subject matter, and the teacher's role. This teacher has developed a style of planning for instruction that includes several interrelated types of planning and that has become more streamlined and automatic with experience. Much of this teacher's interactive teaching consists of routines familiar to the students, thus decreasing the collective information-processing load. During teaching, the teacher attends to and intently processes academic and nonacademic sociocognitive events and cues. These experienced teachers have developed the confidence to depart from a planned course of action when they judge that to be appropriate. They reflect on and analyze the apparent effects of their own teaching and apply the results of these reflections to their future plans and actions. In short, they have become researchers on their own teaching effectiveness.

A decade of research on teachers' thought processes has taught us as much about how to think about teaching as it has about teachers' thinking. Most educators would probably have agreed with the authors of the NIE Panel 6 report that teaching is a complex and cognitively demanding human process (National Institute of Education, 1975a). The research reviewed here has begun to describe in detail the many ways in which teaching is complex, demanding, and uniquely human.

REFERENCES

Ames, R. Teachers' attributions of responsibility: Some unexpected nondefensive effects. *Journal of Educational Psychology, 67,* 668–676.

Ames, R (1982). Teachers' attributions for their own teaching. In J. M. Levine and M. C. Wang (Eds.), *Teacher and student perceptions: Implications for learning.* Hillsdale, NJ: Lawrence Erlbaum.

Anderson, L. M., & Evertson, C. M. (1978). *Classroom organization at the beginning of school: Two case studies.* Paper presented to the American Association of Colleges for Teacher Education, Chicago.

Anderson, R. C. (1977). The notion of schemata and the educational enterprise. In R. C. Anderson, R. Spiro, & W. Montague (Eds.), *Schooling and the acquisition of knowledge.* Hillsdale, NJ: Lawrence Erlbaum.

Anderson, R. C. (1984, November). Some reflections on the acquisition of knowledge. *Educational Researcher, 13,* 5–10.

Bar-Tal, D., & Darom, E. (1979). Pupils' attributions of success and failure. *Child Development, 50,* 264–267.

Beckman, L. (1970). Effects of students' performance on teachers' and observers' attributions of causality. *Journal of Educational Psychology, 61,* 76–82.

Beckman, L. (1973). Teachers' and observers' perceptions of causality for a child's performance. *Journal of Educational Psychology, 65,* 198–204.

Beckman, L. J. (1976). Causal attributions of teachers and parents regarding children's performance. *Psychology in the Schools, 13,* 212–218.

Ben-Peretz, M. (1975). The concept of curriculum potential. *Curriculum Theory Network, 5,* 151–159.

Bishop, A. J., & Whitfield, R. C. (1972). *Situations in teaching.* London: McGraw-Hill.

Bloom, B. S. (1954). The thought processes of students in discussion. In S. J. French (Ed.), *Accent on teaching: Experiments in general education.* New York: Harper Brothers.

Blumenfeld, P. C., Hamilton, V. L., Wessels, K., & Falkner, D. (1977). *"You can," "You should," and "You'd better:" Teacher attributions regarding achievement and social behaviors.* Paper presented at the annual meeting of the American Psychological Association, San Francisco.

Brandt, L. J., Hayden, M. E., & Brophy, J. E. (1975). Teachers' attitudes and ascription of causation. *Journal of Educational Psychology, 67,* 677–682.

Bromme, R. (1982, March). *How to analyze routines in teachers' thinking processes during lesson planning.* Paper presented at the annual meeting of the American Educational Research Association, New York.

Brophy, J. E. (1982). *Research on the self-fulfilling prophecy and teacher expectations* (Research Series No. 119). East Lansing: Michigan State University, Institute for Research on Teaching.

Brophy, J. E., & Rohrkemper, M. M. (1981). The influence of problem ownership on teachers' perceptions of and strategies for coping with problem students. *Journal of Educational Psychology, 73,* 295–311.

Buckley, P. K., & Cooper, J. M. (1978, March). *An ethnographic study of an elementary school teacher's establishment and maintenance of group norms.* Paper presented at the annual meeting of the American Educational Research Association, Toronto, Canada.

Bussis, A. M., Chittenden, F., & Amarel, M. (1976). *Beyond surface curriculum.* Boulder, CO: Westview Press.

Calderhead, J. (1981). A psychological approach to research on teachers' classroom decision making. *British Educational Research Journal, 7,* 51–57.

Calderhead, J. (1983, April). *Research into teachers' and student teachers' cognitions: Exploring the nature of classroom practice.* Paper presented at the annual meeting of the American Educational Research Association, Montreal, Canada.

Carnahan, R. S. (1980). *The effects of teacher planning on classroom processes* (Tech. Rep. No. 541). Madison: Wisconsin R & D Center for Individualized Schooling.

Clark, C. M., & Elmore, J. L. (1979). *Teacher planning in the first weeks of school* (Research Series No. 56). East Lansing: Michigan State University, Institute for Research on Teaching.

Clark, C. M., & Elmore, J. L. (1981). *Transforming curriculum in mathematics, science, and writing: A case study of teacher yearly planning* (Research Series No. 99). East Lansing: Michigan State University, Institute for Research on Teaching.

Clark, C. M., & Peterson, P. L. (1981). Stimulated-recall. In B. R. Joyce, C. C. Brown, & L. Peck (Eds.), *Flexibility in teaching: An excursion into the nature of teaching and training.* New York: Longman.

Clark, C. M., & Yinger, R. J. (1977). Research on teacher thinking. *Curriculum Inquiry, 7*(4), 279–394).

Clark, C. M., & Yinger, R. J. (1979a). Teachers' thinking. In P. L. Peterson & H. J. Walberg (Eds.), *Research on teaching.* Berkeley, CA: McCutchan.

Clark, C. M., & Yinger, R. J. (1979b). *Three studies of teacher planning* (Research Series No. 55). East Lansing: Michigan State University.

Clark, C. M., Yinger, R. J., & Wildfong, S. C. (1978). *Identifying cues for use in studies of teacher judgment* (Research Series No. 23). East Lansing: Institute for Research on Teaching, Michigan State University.

Colker, L. (1982). *Teachers' interactive thoughts about pupil cognition.* Unpublished doctoral dissertation, University of Illinois at Urbana–Champaign.

Cone, R. (1978, March). *Teachers' decisions in managing student behavior: A laboratory simulation of interactive decision-making by teachers.* Paper presented at the annual meeting of the American Educational Research Association, Toronto, Canada.

Connelly, F. M. (1972). The functions of curriculum development. *Interchange, 3,* 161–177.

Conners, R. D. (1978a). *Using stimulated recall in naturalistic settings: Some technical procedures* (Tech. Paper No. 78-2-1). Edmonton, Canada: University of Alberta, Centre for Research in Teaching.

Conners, R. D. (1978b). *An analysis of teacher thought processes, beliefs, and principles during instruction.* Unpublished doctoral dissertation, University of Alberta, Edmonton, Canada.

Cooper, H. M., & Baron, R. M. (1977). Academic expectations and attributed responsibility as predictors of professional teachers' reinforcement behavior. *Journal of Educational Psychology, 69,* 409–418.

Cooper, H. M., & Baron, R. M. (1979). Academic expectations, attributed responsibility, and teachers' reinforcement behavior: A suggested integration of conflicting literatures. *Journal of Educational Psychology, 71,* 274–277.

Cooper, H. M., Baron, R. M., & Lowe, C. A. (1975). The importance of race and social class information in the formation of expectancies about academic performance. *Journal of Educational Psychology, 67,* 312–319.

Cooper, H. M., & Burger, J. M. (1980). How teachers explain students' academic performance: A categorization of free response academic attributions. *American Educational Research Journal, 17,* 95–109.

Corno, L. (1981). Cognitive organizing in classrooms. *Curriculum Inquiry, 11,* 359–377.

Covington, M. V., Spratt, M. F., & Omelich, C. L. (1980). Is effort enough, or does diligence count too? Student and teacher reactions to effort stability in failure. *Journal of Educational Psychology, 72,* 717–729.

Creemers, B. P. M., & Westerhof, K. (1982). *Routinization of instructive and management behavior of teachers* (research paper). Haren, The Netherlands: Educational Research Institute in the North.

Crist, J., Marx, R. W., & Peterson, P. L. (1974). *Teacher behavior in the organizational domain* (Report submitted to the National Institute of Education). Stanford, CA: Stanford Center for R & D in Teaching.

Dahllof, U., & Lundgren, U. P. (1970). *Macro- and micro approaches combined for curriculum process analysis: A Swedish educational field project.* Göteborg, Sweden: University of Göteborg, Institute of Education. (Mimeo)

Darley, J. M., & Fazio, R. H. (1980). Expectancy confirmation processes arising in the social interaction sequence. *American Psychologist, 35,* 867–881.

De Corte, E., & Lowyck, J. (1980). *Analysis of cognitive processes in teaching behavior* (Report No. 24). Leuven, Belgium: Katholieke Universiteit te Leuven, Department Pedagogische Wetenschappen.

Domingo-Llacuna, E. A. (1976). The effect of pupil race, social class, speech and ability on teacher stereotypes and attributions (Doctoral dissertation, University of Illinois at Urbana-Champaign, 1976). *Dissertation Abstracts International, 37,* 2737–2738. (University Microfilms No. 76-24, 072)

Doyle, W. (1977a). Learning the classroom environment: An ecological analysis. *Journal of Teacher Education, 28,* 51–55.

Doyle, W. (1977b). Paradigms for research on teacher effectiveness. *Review of Research in Education, 5,* 163–198.

Doyle, W. (1979). Making managerial decisions in classrooms. In D. L.

Duke (Ed.), *Classroom management* (Yearbook of the National Society for the Study of Education). Chicago: University of Chicago Press.

Duffy, G. (1977). *A study of teacher conceptions of reading.* Paper presented at the National Reading Conference, New Orleans.

Dunkin, M. J., & Biddle, B. J. (1974). *The study of teaching.* New York: Holt, Rinehart & Winston.

Dweck, C. S., Davidson, W., Nelson, S., & Enna, B. (1978). 1. Sex differences in learned helplessness: 2. The contingencies of evaluative feedback in the classroom; 3. An experimental analysis. *Developmental Psychology, 14,* 268-276.

Eisner, E. W. (1967). Educational objectives: Help or hindrance? *School Review, 75,* 250-260.

Eisner, E. W., & Vallance, E. (1974). *Conflicting conceptions of curriculum.* Berkeley, CA: McCutchan.

Elbaz, F. (1980). *The teacher's "practical knowledge": A case study.* Unpublished doctoral dissertation, University of Toronto.

Elbaz, F. (1981). The teacher's "practical knowledge": Report of a case study. *Curriculum Inquiry, 11,* 43-71.

Elbaz, F. (1983). *Teacher thinking: A study of practical knowledge.* New York: Nichols Publishing.

Elliot, J. (1976). *Developing hypotheses about classrooms from teachers' practical constructs.* Grand Forks: North Dakota Study Group.

Ericcson, K. A., & Simon, H. A. (1980). Verbal reports as data. *Psychological Review, 87,* 215-251.

Favor-Lydecker, A. (1981, April). *Teacher planning of social studies instructional units.* Paper presented at the annual meeting of the American Educational Research Association, Los Angeles.

Feuquay, J. P. (1979). Teachers' self-attributions and their projections of student attributions under varying conditions (Doctoral dissertation, Oklahoma State University, 1979). *Dissertation Abstracts International, 40,* 4487 (University Microfilms No. 8003570)

Fogarty, J. L., Wang, M. C., & Creek, R. (1982, March). *A descriptive study of experienced and novice teachers' interactive instructional decision processes.* Paper presented at the annual meeting of the American Educational Research Association, New York City.

Frieze, I. H. (1976). Causal attributions and information-seeking to explain success and failure. *Journal of Research in Personality, 10,* 293-305.

Goodlad, J., & Klein, M. F. (1970). *Behind the classroom door.* Worthington, OH: Charles A. Jones.

Hammond, K. R. (1971). Computer graphics as an aid to learning. *Science, 172,* 903-908.

Hanes, B. F. (1979). Causal attributions by teacher-trainees for success and failure outcomes of elementary students labeled normal and gifted (Doctoral dissertation, Oklahoma State University, 1979). *Dissertation Abstracts International, 40,* 3198-31995S. (University Microfilms No. 7928212)

Heider, F. (1958). *The pscychology of interpersonal relations.* New York: Wiley.

Heller, K. A., & Parsons, J. E. (1981). Sex differences in teachers' evaluative feedback and students' expectancies for success in mathematics. *Child Development, 52,* 1015–1019.

Hill, J., Yinger, R. J., & Robbins, D. (1981, April). *Instructional planning in a developmental preschool.* Paper presented at the annual meeting of the American Educational Research Association, Los Angeles.

Housner, L. D., & Griffey, D. C. (1983, April). *Teacher cognition: Differences in planning and interactive decision making between experienced and inexperienced teachers.* Paper presented at the annual meeting of the American Educational Research Association, Montreal, Canada.

Ignatovich, F. R., Cusick, P. A., & Ray, J. E. (1979). *Value/belief patterns of teachers and those administrators engaged in attempts to influence teaching* (Research Series No. 43). East Lansing: Michigan State University, Institute for Research on Teaching.

Jackson, P. W. (1966). *The way teaching is.* Washington, DC: National Education Association.

Jackson, P. W. (1968). *Life in classrooms.* New York: Holt, Rinehart & Winston.

Janesick, V. (1977). *An ethnographic study of a teacher's classroom perspective.* Unpublished doctoral dissertation, Michigan State University, East Lansing.

Johnson, T. J., Feigenbaum, R., & Weiby, M. (1964). Some determinants and consequences of the teacher's perception of causation. *Journal of Educational Psychology, 55,* 237–246.

Jones, E. E., & Nisbett, R. E. (1971). *The actor and observer: Divergent perceptions of the causes of behavior.* Morristown, NJ: General Learning Press.

Joyce, B. R. (1978–1979). Toward a theory of information processing in teaching. *Educational Research Quarterly, 3*(4), 66–77.

Joyce, B. R., & Harootunian, B. (1964). Teaching as problem solving. *Journal of Teacher Education, 15,* 420–427.

Kelly, G. A. (1955). *The psychology of personal constructs* (2 vols.). New York: W. W. Norton.

King, L. H. (1980). *Student thought processes and the expectancy effect* (Research Rep. No. 80-1-8). Churchlands, Perth, Australia: Churchlands College of Advanced Education.

Lowyck, J. (1980). *A process analysis of teaching* (Report No. 21). Leuven, Belgium: Katholieke Universiteit te Leuven, Departement Pedagogische Wetenschappen.

MacKay, D. A., & Marland, P. W. (1978, March). *Thought processes of teachers.* Paper presented at the annual meeting of the American Educational Research Association, Toronto, Canada.

Marland, P. W. (1977). *A study of teachers' interactive thoughts.* Unpublished doctoral dissertation, University of Alberta, Edmonton, Canada.

Marx, R. W., & Peterson, P. L. (1981). The nature of teacher decision making. In B. R. Joyce, C. C. Brown, & L. Peck (Eds.), *Flexibility in teaching: An excursion into the nature of teaching and training.* New York: Longman.

McCutcheon, G. (1980). How do elementary school teachers plan? The nature of planning and influences on it. *Elementary School Journal, 81,* 4–23.

McLeod, M. A. (1981). *The identification of intended learning outcomes by early childhood teachers: An exploratory study.* Unpublished doctoral dissertation, University of Alberta, Edmonton, Canada.

McNair, K. (1978 1979). Capturing inflight decisions. *Educational Research Quarterly, 3*(4), 26 42.

Medway, F. J. (1979). Causal attributions for school-related problems: Teacher perceptions and teacher feedback. *Journal of Educational Psychology, 71,* 809-818.

Meyer, W. U. (1979). Academic expectations, attributed responsibility, and teacher's reinforcement behavior: A comment on Cooper and Baron, with some additional data. *Journal of Educational Psychology, 71,* 269-273.

Morine, G., & Vallance, E. (1975). *Special study B: A study of teacher and pupil perceptions of classroom interaction* (Tech. Rep. No. 75-11-6). San Francisco: Far West Laboratory.

Morine-Dershimer, G. (1977, April). *What's in a plan? Stated and unstated plans for lessons.* Paper presented at the annual meeting of the American Educational Research Association, New York.

Morine-Dershimer, G. (1978-1979). Planning and classroom reality: An in-depth look. *Educational Research Quarterly, 3*(4), 83-99.

Morine-Dershimer, G. (1979). *Teacher plan and classroom reality: The South Bay study: Part 4* (Research Series No. 60). East Lansing: Michigan State University, Institute for Research on Teaching.

Morine-Dershimer, G., & Vallance, E. (1976). *Teacher planning* (Beginning Teacher Evaluation Study, Special Report C). San Francisco: Far West Laboratory.

Munby, H. (1982). The place of teachers' beliefs in research on teacher thinking and decision making, and an alternative methodology. *Instructional Science, 11,* 201-225.

Munby, H. (1983, April). *A qualitative study of teachers' beliefs and principles.* Paper presented at the annual meeting of the American Educational Research Association, Montreal.

National Institute of Education. (1975a). *Teaching as clinical information processing* (Report of Panel 6, National Conference on Studies in Teaching). Washington, DC: National Institute of Education.

National Institute of Education. (1975b). *Theory development.* (Report of Panel 10, National Conference on Studies in Teaching). Washington, DC: National Institute of Education.

Neale, D. C., Pace, A. J., & Case, A. B. (1983, April). *The influence of training, experience, and organizational environment on teachers' use of the systematic planning model.* Paper presented at the annual meeting of the American Educational Research Association, Montreal.

Newell, A., & Simon, H. A. (1972). *Human problem solving.* Englewood Cliffs, NJ: Prentice-Hall.

Nisbett, R. E., & Ross, L. (1980). *Human inference: Strategies and shortcomings of social judgment.* Englewood Cliffs, NJ: Prentice-Hall.

Nisbett, R. E., & Wilson, T. D. (1977). Telling more than we can know: Verbal reports on mental processes. *Psychological Review, 84,* 231-259.

Olson, J. K. (1980). *Innovative doctrines and practical dilemmas: A case study of curriculum translation.* Unpublished doctoral dissertation. University of Birmingham, England.

Olson, J. K. (1981). Teacher influence in the classroom. *Instructional Science, 10,* 259-275.

Peterson, P. L., & Barger, S. A. (1984). Attribution theory and teacher expectancy. In J. B. Dusek (Ed.), *Teacher expectancies* (pp. 159-184). Hillsdale, NJ: Lawrence Erlbaum.

Peterson, P. L., & Clark, C. M. (1978). Teachers' reports of their cognitive processes during teaching. *American Educational Research Journal, 15,* 555-565.

Peterson, P. L., Marx, R. W., & Clark, C. M. (1978). Teacher planning, teacher behavior, and student achievement. *American Educational Research Journal, 15,* 417-432.

Peterson, P. L., Swing, S. R., Braverman, M. T., & Buss, R. (1982). Students' aptitudes and their reports of cognitive processes during direct instruction. *Journal of Educational Psychology, 74,* 535-547.

Peterson, P. L., Swing, S. R., Stark, K. D., & Wass, G. A. (1983, April). *Students' reports of their cognitive processes and affective thoughts during classroom instruction.* Paper presented at the annual meeting of the American Educational Research Association, Montreal.

Peterson, P. L., & Walberg, H. J. (Eds.). (1979). *Research on teaching: Concepts, findings, and implications.* Berkeley, CA: McCutchan.

Popham, J. W., & Baker, E. L. (1970). *Systematic instruction.* Englewood Cliffs, NJ: Prentice-Hall.

Posner, G. (1981). New developments in curricular research: It's the thought that counts. *The Researcher* (Newsletter of the Northeastern Educational Research Association), *19,* 25-55.

Prawat, R. S., Byers, J. L., & Anderson, A. H. (1983). An attributional analysis of teachers' affective reactions to student success and failure. *American Educational Research Journal, 1,* 137-152.

Pylypiw, J. (1974). *A description of classroom curriculum development.* Unpublished doctoral dissertation, University of Alberta, Edmonton, Canada.

Rappoport, L., & Summers, D. A. (1973). *Human judgment and social interaction.* New York: Holt, Rinehart & Winston.

Raths, J. D. (1971). Teaching without specific objectives. *Educational Leadership, 28,* 714-720.

Rosenshine, B. V., & Furst, N. (1973). The use of direct observation to study teaching. In R. M. W. Travers (Ed.), *Second handbook of research on teaching.* Chicago: Rand McNally.

Ross, L., Bierbrauer, G., & Polly, S. (1974). Attribution of educational outcomes by professional and nonprofessional instructors. *Journal of Personality and Social Psychology, 29,* 609-618.

Rumelhart, D. E. (1980). Schemata: The building blocks of cognition. In R. J. Spiro, B. C. Bruce, & W. F. Brewer (Eds.), *Theoretical issues in reading comprehension: Perspectives from cognitive psychology, linguistics, artificial intelligence, and education.* Hillsdale, NJ: Lawrence Erlbaum.

Sardo, D. (1982, October). *Teacher planning styles in the middle school.* Paper presented to the Eastern Educational Research Association, Ellenville, NY.

Semmel, D. S. (1977, April). *The effects of training on teacher decision making*. Paper presented at the annual meeting of the American Educational Research Association, New York City. (ERIC Document Reproduction Service No. ED 138 558)

Semmel, M. I., Brady, M. E., & Semmel, D. S. (1976). *The development of oral reading prompting skills in a CATTS–CBTE program for pre-service teachers of the mildly handicapped* (Final Rep. No. 53.5). Bloomington: Indiana University, Center for Innovation in Teaching the Handicapped. (ERIC Document Reproduction Service No. ED 162 468)

Shavelson, R. J. (1973). *The basic teaching skill: Decision making* (R & D Memorandum No. 104). Stanford, CA: Stanford University, School of Education, Center for R & D in Teaching.

Shavelson, R. J. (1976). Teachers' decision making. In N. L. Gage (Ed.), *The psychology of teaching methods* (Yearbook of the National Society for the Study of Education). Chicago: University of Chicago Press.

Shavelson, R. J., Atwood, N. K., & Borko, H. (1977). Experiments on some factors contributing to teachers' pedagogical decisions. *Cambridge Journal of Education, 7*, 51–70.

Shavelson, R. J., & Stern, P. (1981). Research on teachers' pedagogical thoughts, judgments, decisions, and behavior. *Review of Educational Research, 51*, 455–498.

Shroyer, J. C. (1981). *Critical moments in the teaching of mathematics: What makes teaching difficult?* Unpublished doctoral dissertation, Michigan State University, East Lansing.

Shulman, L. S., & Elstein, A. S. (1975). Studies of problem solving, judgment, and decision making: Implications for educational research. In F. N. Kerlinger (Ed.), *Review of Research in Education, 3*, 5–42.

Shultz, J., & Florio, S. (1979). Stop and freeze: The negotiation of social and physical space in a kindergarten/first grade classroom. *Anthropology and Education Quarterly, 10*, 166–181.

Silverstein, M. (1978). An attributional analysis of teachers' evaluative judgements (Doctoral dissertation, University of Rhode Island, 1978). *Dissertation Abstracts International, 39*, 1055–1056C. (University Microfilm No. 7813272)

Simon, H. A. (1957). *Models of man.* New York: Wiley.

Smith, E. L., & Sendelbach, N. B. (1979). *Teacher intentions for science instruction and their antecedents in program materials.* Paper presented at the annual meeting of the American Educational Research Association, San Francisco.

Smith, J. K. (1977, October). *Teacher planning for instruction* (Report No. 12). Chicago: CEMREL Studies of Educative Processes.

Snow, R. E. (1972). *A model teacher training system: An overview* (R & D Memorandum No. 92). Stanford University, School of Education, Center for R & D in Teaching. (ERIC Document Reproduction Service No. ED 066 437.)

Staton, J. (1982). *Dialogue journal writing as a communicative event* (Vol. 1). Washington, DC: Georgetown University Center for Applied Linguistics. (Mimeo)

Sutcliffe, J., & Whitfield, R. (1979). Classroom-based teaching decisions. In J. Eggleston (Ed.), *Teacher decision-making in the classroom: A collection of papers*. London: Routledge & Kegan Paul.

Taylor, P. H. (1970). *How teachers plan their courses*. Slough, Berkshire, England: National Foundation for Educational Research.

Tetlock, P. E. (1980). Explaining teacher explanations of pupil performance: A self-presentation interpretation. *Social Psychology Quarterly, 43,* 283-290.

Tikunoff, W. J., & Ward, B. A. (1978). *A naturalistic study of the initiation of students into three classroom social systems* (Report A-78-11). San Francisco: Far West Laboratory.

Toomey, R. (1977). Teachers' approaches to curriculum planning. *Curriculum Inquiry, 7,* 121-129.

Travers, R. M. W. (Ed.). (1973). *Second handbook of research on teaching*. Chicago: Rand McNally.

Tuckwell, N. B. (1980a). *Content analysis of stimulated recall protocols* (Tech. Paper No. 80-2-2). Edmonton, Canada: University of Alberta, Centre for Research in Teaching.

Tuckwell, N. B. (1980b). *Stimulated recall: Theoretical perspectives and practical and technical considerations* (Tech. Rep. No. 80-2-3). Edmonton, Canada: University of Alberta, Centre for Research in Teaching.

Tyler, R. W. (1950). *Basic principles of curriculum and instruction*. Chicago: University of Chicago Press.

Weiner, B. (Ed.). (1974). *Achievement motivation and attribution theory*. Morristown, NJ: General Learning Press.

Weiner, B., Frieze, I. H., Kukla, A., Reed, L., Rest, S., & Rosenbaum, R. M. (1971). *Perceiving the causes of success and failure*. Morristown, NJ: General Learning Press.

Weiner, B., & Kukla, A. (1970). An attributional analysis of achievement motivation. *Journal of Personality and Social Psychology, 15,* 1-20.

Wiley, M. G., & Eskilson, A. (1978). Why did you learn in school today? Teachers' perceptions of causality. *Sociology of Education, 51,* 261-269.

Wise, R. I. (1976). The use of objectives in curriculum planning. *Curriculum Theory Network, 5,* 280-289.

Wodlinger, M. G. (1980). *A study of teacher interactive decision making*. Unpublished doctoral dissertation, University of Alberta, Edmonton, Canada.

Yinger, R. J. (1977). *A study of teacher planning: Description and theory development using ethnographic and information processing methods*. Unpublished doctoral dissertation, Michigan State University, East Lansing.

Yinger, R. J. (1979). Routines in teacher planning. *Theory into Practice, 18,* 163-169.

Yinger, R. J., & Clark, C. M. (1981). *Reflective journal writing: Theory and practice* (Occasional Paper No. 50). East Lansing: Michigan State University, Institute for Research on Teaching.

Yinger, R. J., & Clark, C. M. (1982). *Understanding teachers' judgments about instruction: The task, the method, and the meaning* (Research

Series No. 121). East Lansing: Michigan State University, Institute for Research on Teaching.

Yinger, R. J., & Clark, C. M. (1983). *Self-reports of teacher judgment.* (Research Series No. 134). East Lansing: Michigan State University, Institute for Research on Teaching.

Yinger, R. J., & Clark, C. M. (1985). *Using personal documents to study teacher thinking* (Occasional paper No. 84). East Lansing: Michigan State University, Institute for Research on Teaching.

Zahorik, J. A. (1970). The effects of planning on teaching. *Elementary School Journal, 71,* 143–151.

Zahorik, J. A. (1975). Teachers' planning models. *Educational Leadership, 33,* 134–139.

INDEX